MUSIC OF THE TWENTIETH CENTURY

AN ANTHOLOGY

BRYAN R. SIMMS
University of Southern California

SCHIRMER BOOKS
A Division of Macmillan, Inc.
NEW YORK

Copyright © 1986 by Schirmer Books
A Division of Macmillan, Inc.

All rights reserved. No part of this book may be reproduced or transmitted in any form or by any means, electronic or mechanical, including photocopying, recording, or by any information storage and retrieval system, without permission in writing from the Publisher.

Schirmer Books
A Division of Macmillan, Inc.
866 Third Avenue, New York, N. Y. 10022

Library of Congress Catalog Card Number: 85-754459

Printed in the United States of America

printing number

8 9 10

Library of Congress Cataloging-in-Publication Data
Main entry under title.

Music of the twentieth century.

1. Musical analysis—Music collections. 2. Music appreciation—Music collections. 3. Music—20th century.
I. Simms, Bryan R. II. Title: Music of the 20th century.
MT6.5.M93 1986 85-754459
ISBN 0-02-873020-8

CONTENTS

CONTENTS BY COMPOSER

PREFACE

The works contained in this anthology provide the student of modern music with a representative sample of the major musical styles of this century. These pieces and their place in the history of twentieth-century music are discussed in *Music of the Twentieth Century: Style and Structure* by Bryan R. Simms (Schirmer Books, 1986), for which this anthology serves as a companion volume.

Diversity has been a primary goal in choosing the contents that follow. As many different composers, genres, and styles as possible are presented, and there is a balance of works from both the early and recent decades of the century.

The contents are organized by medium or by genre and, within each of these categories, by chronology of composition. Music for piano—the first subdivision—has continued in the twentieth century to occupy the central position that it held in the nineteenth. The selections by Satie, Debussy, Ravel, Bartók, and Milhaud are in the genre of the character piece—a concise movement, that is, which projects a particular mood, emotion, or programmatic idea. Schoenberg's Piano Piece, op. 23, no. 4, is an abstract atonal conception; Cowell's *The Banshee,* an experimental study in sound in which the instrument is played in an entirely novel way. The finale of Prokofiev's Seventh Piano Sonata—one of his most avant-garde works—mobilizes asymmetrical rhythms and irregular division of the measure for its impetuous effect. The two works by Cage exemplify his experiments with "prepared" piano and with the chance selection of sounds and silences.

Works for solo voice by Fauré, Berg, Ives, and Hindemith continue the nineteenth-century conception of the song, but they contain many new stylistic ideas. Berg's "Warm die Lüfte" is his earliest atonal composition, Ives's "Charlie Rutlage" uses spoken narration, and Hindemith's song from *Das Marienleben* combines this composer's incipient neoclassicism with a chromatic style of harmony and melody. The remaining selections for solo voice are examples of an important new genre in the twentieth century: song-like compositions accompanied by small and diverse chamber orchestras or ensembles. Berio's adaptation of "Black is the Color of My True Love's Hair" adds to the repertory of artistic folk song arrangements which had their greatest popularity early in the century. Davies's "Country Dance" from *Eight Songs for a Mad King* allies the ensemble song to theatric elements of presentation.

Selections from opera and ballet constitute the next category. The excerpts from Stravinsky's *Petrushka* and Shostakovich's *Lady Macbeth* are brilliant orchestral works which can be used as independent concert pieces. Movements from two of the outstanding choral compositions of the century—Stravinsky's Mass and Webern's Second Cantata—are given as examples of divergent styles of modern choral writing.

The emphasis upon clarity and economy in music early in the twentieth century brought about a great revival of chamber music. Selections by Schoenberg, Crumb, and Rochberg illustrate three distinct approaches to writing for string quartet. Schoenberg's Fourth String Quartet is a twelve-tone work which is otherwise traditional in form. Rochberg's Sixth String Quartet is an eclectic piece that pays homage to several of his forebears. Crumb's *Black Angels* calls for the instruments of the quartet to be amplified and for the players to produce many unorthodox sounds. Varèse's *Octandre* and Stockhausen's *Kreuzspiel* are for mixed chamber groups, and Reich's *Clapping Music* uses no instruments at all other than the hands of two performers.

All works having texts in foreign languages are provided with new translations by the compiler. The bibliography refers readers to the chapter in *Music of the Twentieth Century: Style and Structure* in which a further discussion of the music may be found. Other bibliographic entries are limited in general to writings in English. The discography emphasizes recent commercial recordings, cassette tapes, and compact discs that are available in the United States. The dates at the end of these discographic citations are those of issue.

PART I **MUSIC FOR PIANO**

♦1♦

Erik Satie (1866–1925)

Saraband no. 1 (1887)

Satie's three Sarabands for piano are among his earliest compositions, but they set forth a style to which he would be faithful for the remainder of his career. The pieces are disarmingly simple in texture, delicate in sonority, and repetitive in construction.

The harmonies of the first Saraband rely upon unresolved sevenths and ninths for their pungent sonority—a feature that we associate with the later music of Satie's friend Debussy. Satie was perhaps indebted for this colorful harmonic practice to Emmanuel Chabrier, whose comic opera *Le roi malgré lui* contains similar passages. Satie heard this work—by which he was greatly inspired—in Paris only months before composing the Sarabands.

Bibliography

Music of the Twentieth Century, Chapter 8.
Myers, Rollo H. *Erik Satie*, pp. 67–93. London, 1948.
Wehmeyer, Grete. *Satie.* Regensburg, 1974, passim.

Discography

Piano Music of Erik Satie, vol. 3. Aldo Ciccolini, piano. Angel S 36485 (1968).
Piano Music of Erik Satie. Frank Glazer, piano. Vox SVBX 5422 (1968).
Piano Music by Erik Satie. John McCabe, piano. Saga 5387 (1974).
Satie: Selected Piano Music. Laurence Allix, piano. Musical Heritage Society MHS 1978-79 (1975).
Piano Music of Satie. Daniel Varsano, piano. Columbia M 36694 (1981).

Copyright © 1911 by Editions Salabert. All rights reserved. Used by permission of G. Schirmer, Inc., U.S. agent.

30
p
f
p
35
p
f
40
cresc.
f
p
45
50
pp
55
p
60

65
pp
70
75
80
p
85
90
pp
p
95
pp
100
ralentir

• 2 •

Claude Debussy (1862–1918)

Pour le piano *(1894–1901):*
Saraband

Debussy composed this Saraband in 1894 as one of a group of character pieces for piano which he called "Images." The Saraband was revised in 1901 and placed as the second movement of the collection *Pour le piano.* It was later orchestrated by Maurice Ravel.

Although a relatively early work, the Saraband exemplifies Debussy's mature style in its elegant melodiousness and subtle exploitation of the sonority of the piano. The tonic key of C-sharp minor is treated with great freedom and is colored by swathes of pentatonic motion, quartal harmony, and unresolved seventh chords moving in parallel.

The original version of the Saraband was published most recently in 1977 by Theodore Presser.

Bibliography

Music of the Twentieth Century, Chapter 8.

Lockspeiser, Edward. *Debussy.* 5th ed. Master Musicians Series. London, 1980.

Vallas, Léon. *Claude Debussy: His Life and Works,* pp. 155–57, 275. Trans. Maire and Grace O'Brien. Oxford, 1933.

Discography

Piano Music of Debussy. Philippe Entremont, piano. Columbia MS 6567 (1964).

Gina Bachauer, piano. Mercury SRI 75139 (1965).

Michel Béroff, piano. Angel S 36874 (1972).

Zoltán Kocsis, piano. Philips 412118-2PH (compact disc, 1984).

Paris: E. Fromont, 1901.

25
pp
30
mf
p
pp
Animez un peu
35
mp
p très soutenu
40
p
Au mouvt
3
f
45
3
f

50
p
plus p
55
mf
cresc.
f
ff
60
p
più p
65
retenu
p dim.
plus p
70
pp
ppp
m.d.

◆3◆

Maurice Ravel (1875–1937)

Jeux d'eau *(1901)*

In his "Autobiographical Sketch" printed in the *Revue musicale* in December 1938, Maurice Ravel underscores the importance of *Jeux d'eau* in his future development as a composer:

> *Jeux d'eau*, which appeared in 1901, is at the source of all the pianistic innovations that have been noted in my work. This piece, inspired by the sound of water and by the musical sounds made by fountains, waterfalls, and streams, is based on two motives in the manner of the first movement of a sonata, but without a classical tonal plan.

The title of this work and its effervescent arpeggios were probably suggested to Ravel by Liszt's "Les jeux d'eaux à la Villa d'Este" from the third *Année de pèlerinage* (1877). The poet Henri de Régnier added this epigraph to Ravel's score: "River god laughing from the water which tickles him."

The virtuosic writing for piano of *Jeux d'eau* and its watery images recur in Ravel's work, notably in "A Boat on the Ocean" from *Miroirs* and "Ondine" from *Gaspard de la nuit*.

Bibliography

Music of the Twentieth Century, Chapter 8.

Orenstein, Arbie. *Ravel: Man and Musician*, pp. 154, 213–14, and passim. New York, London, 1975.

Ravel, Maurice. "Esquisse autobiographique." *Revue musicale*, 19 (1938), 211–15.

Discography

Maurice Ravel: The Complete Works for Solo Piano. Philippe Entremont, piano. Columbia D3M 33311 (1975).

Maurice Ravel: Piano Music. Paul Badura-Skoda, piano. Musical Heritage Society MHS 4148 (1979).

Jean-Philippe Collard, piano. EMI 2C 167/73.025–73.027 (1980).

Gilels Live at Carnegie Hall. Emil Gilels, piano. Musical Heritage Society MHS 4369–4370 (1981).

New York: G. Schirmer, 1907. Edited and revised by Rafael Joseffy.

8
8
8
ff
f
mf
rapido

pp una corda
tre corde
pp subito
una corda
tre corde
trem.
ff

27
28
rit.
a tempo
29
30
pp una corda
31
l.h.
l.
33
8
p
tre corde

35
36
37
38
39
rapido
il canto un poco marcato
p
(sopra)

40
41
mp
42
8
43
8
f
44
8
cresc. e accel.

45
46
ff
47
48
lunga
trem.
fff
glissando
49
50
Ped.

Tempo I
p
Ped.
pp
tre corde
f
p una corda

57
tre corde
Ped.
59
60
mf
61
f
rall. leggermente

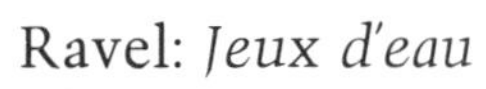

return to (a) (1st idea)
Tempo I
62
pp una corda
G# pedal
EM 6 5
64
65
mf
66
pp
68
69

70
ppp
72
rapido molto
tre corde
ppp
fff
f
mf
dim.
p
rall.
73
Un poco più lento del principio
rall.

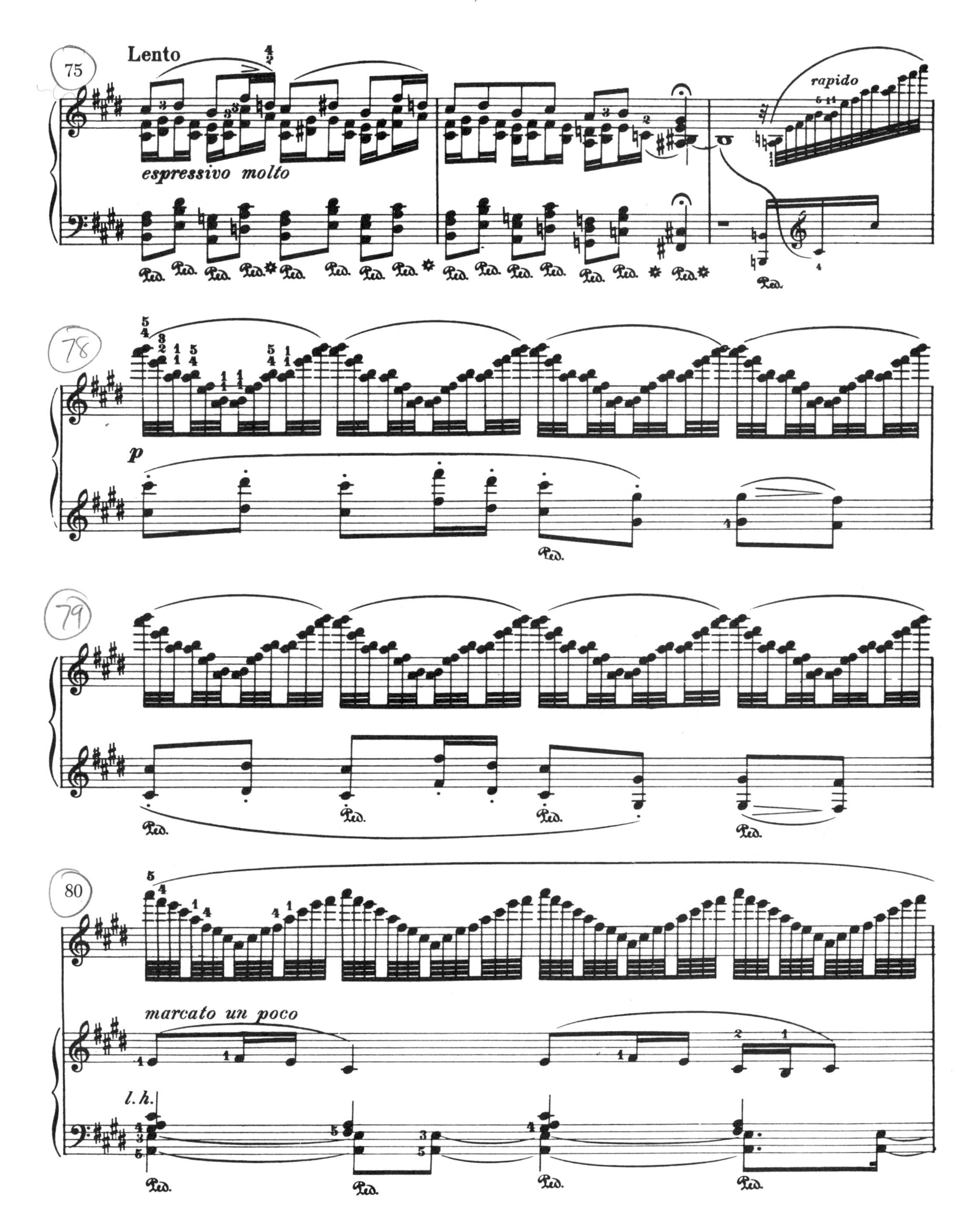
75
Lento
espressivo molto
rapido
78
p
79
80
marcato un poco
l.h.

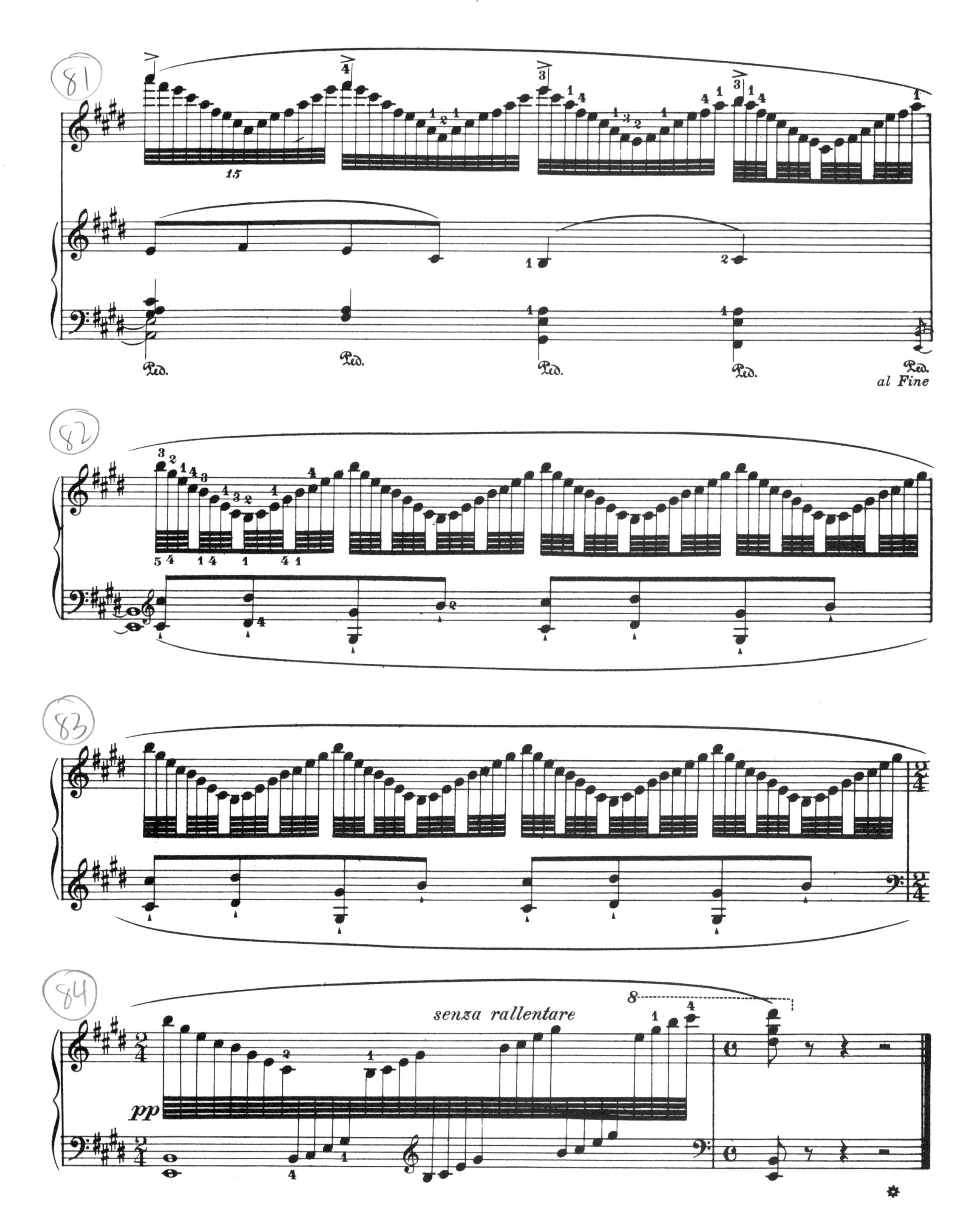
81
15
Ped.
Ped.
Ped.
Ped.
Ped.
al Fine
82
83
84
senza rallentare
8
pp

◆ 4 ◆

Béla Bartók (1881–1945)

Fourteen Bagatelles for piano, op. 6 (1908): nos. 1, 4, 8, 14

Bartók's Fourteen Bagatelles are character pieces in the concise and abstract style that characterizes his music from the time of their composition through the 1920s. In the Introduction to his *Masterpieces for the Piano* (1945), he describes their idiom as a "reaction to the exuberance of the romantic piano music of the nineteenth century, a style stripped of all inessential decorative elements, deliberately using only the most restricted technical means."

The first Bagatelle contains conflicting key signatures in its two staves. According to Bartók, this conflict shows the "absurdity" of key signatures in certain kinds of contemporary music. He states that the work is in a "Phrygian-colored C major." Bagatelle no. 4 is a harmonization of a folk song that Bartók recorded in 1907 in the region of Tolna in southern Hungary. The eighth Bagatelle is one of the most experimental of the entire set in its free use of chromatic pitches and nondiatonic harmonies. Bartók considered it to express the key of G minor.

Bagatelle no. 14 is a grotesque waltz, subtitled "My dancing sweetheart." It contains a melodic figure introduced in measures 9–12 that Bartók had earlier used to signify his friend Stefi Geyer. Geyer had broken off their relationship shortly before the Bagatelles were written.

Bibliography

Music of the Twentieth Century, Chapter 9.

Antokoletz, Elliott. "The Musical Language of Bartók's *14 Bagatelles* for Piano." *Tempo*, 137 (1981), 8–16. Material from this article is elaborated on in idem, *The Music of Béla Bartók*. Berkeley, Los Angeles, London, 1984.

Bartók, Béla. "Introduction to *Béla Bartók Masterpieces for the Piano.*" In *Essays*, pp. 432–33. Ed. Benjamin Suchoff. New York, 1976.

Forte, Allen. *Contemporary Tone-Structures*, pp. 74–90. New York, 1955.

Stevens, Halsey. *The Life and Music of Béla Bartók*, pp. 111–12. Rev. ed. London, Oxford, New York, 1964.

Discography

Béla Bartók Complete Edition. Kornél Zempléni, piano. Hungaroton LPX 1299 (196–).

Gyorgy Sandor, piano. Vox SVBX 5247 (1961).

Robert Silverman, piano. Orion ORS 74152; Orion 650 (cassette tape) (1974).

Robert Hagopian, piano. Etcetera 1012 (digital, 1983).

1.

Budapest: Rozsnyai Károly, 1909.

4.

Grave 𝅗𝅥 69.
3/4
ff legatissimo

5
p poco cresc.
p cresc. molto
ff

10
p poco cresc.
p cresc. molto
ff

8.

Andante sostenuto ♩/54-60.
p
5
10
cresc.
p
Sostenuto
15
espr. ♩/42-46
pp
pp
p

20
poco agitato
f
poco rit.
Più sostenuto
mp
25
dim.
Ritenuto
p dolciss.
30

14.

Introduction (m. 1-8)
Presto
f con fuoco
5
D
D
D
D
10
sf
simile
D M7
G 6
sf
15
20
sf
Tritones
25
ritard. molto
G A B C# Eb = Whole Tone
30
a tempo
35
sf
C

40
sf
45
poco a poco accel.
mf
50
55
4
60
cresc. molto
dim.
65
ritard.
Tempo I
3
70
3
mf
p

75
80
85
f poco largo ♩/120
dim.
90
poco a poco accel.
a tempo
f
p
F
95
100
105

110
115
f poco largo
dim.
p a tempo
120
125
dim.
accel.
130
pp
cresc.
135
160
ff dim.
140
176
145
poco a poco rit.
pp

150
al 144
pp volante
155
poco a poco
160
cresc.
165
170
f
7
175
8
cresc. molto

180
185
190
195
200
205
210
215
sf
ff
dim.
p
pp
mf
fff marcatissimo
1
2

• 5 •

Darius Milhaud (1892–1974)

Saudades do Brazil *(1920):*
"Botafogo"

Darius Milhaud's fascination with dance music of Latin America began in 1917 during a sojourn in Rio de Janeiro, where he served as an assistant to Paul Claudel, then France's ambassador to Brazil. After he returned to France, Milhaud recreated the lazy syncopations of the *maxixe, lundú,* and *samba* in his collection of twelve dances for piano, *Saudades do Brazil.*

"Botafogo"—like each of the dances—is named after a location near Rio. This work is an example of polytonality, with which Milhaud experimented at this period. In the outer sections, the main melody in the right hand outlines the key of F-sharp minor, which is superimposed above an accompaniment in F minor.

The *Saudades* were subsequently orchestrated by the composer.

Bibliography

Music of the Twentieth Century, Chapter 9.
Milhaud, Darius. *Notes Without Music.* Trans. Donald Evans, ed. Rollo H. Myers. New York, 1952.

Discography

William Bolcom, piano. Nonesuch H 71316 (1975).

Copyright © 1922 by Editions Max Eschig. All rights reserved. Used by permission of Associated Music Publishers, Inc., U.S. agent.

Ral.
Mouvt du début
Sans ralentir

◆6◆

Arnold Schoenberg (1874–1951)

Five Piano Pieces, op. 23 (1920–23): Piece no. 4

The Piano Piece, op. 23, no. 4, is Schoenberg's last atonal work prior to his embarking upon the twelve-tone method of composition. Atonal music, which he composed from about 1908, is predominantly dissonant and lacks traditional key. It is unified instead by motivic development and by varied recurrences of sets of pitches.

Schoenberg composed the first fourteen measures of this piece in July 1920, at about the same time that he completed the first and second pieces of opus 23. These first two pieces were performed by Eduard Steuermann in a concert of the Society for Private Musical Performances later in 1920. Schoenberg returned to the fourth piece nearly three years later, and it was completed in February 1923, after he had made his earliest essays in twelve-tone composition. He did not use this method in this piano piece, however, but followed instead a method that he termed "composing with tones of the motive." According to this approach, the pitches of basic motives introduced at the beginning of a work return systematically in varied forms in both lines and chords.

Opus 23 was completed by the addition of two other pieces composed in 1922 and 1923. These two works are among Schoenberg's earliest examples of serial composition.

Bibliography

Music of the Twentieth Century, Chapters 2 and 7.

Forte, Allen. "Sets and Nonsets in Schoenberg's Atonal Music." *Perspectives of New Music*, 11 (1972), 43–64.

Graziano, John. "Serial Procedures in Schoenberg's Opus 23." *Current Musicology*, 13 (1972), 58–63.

Maegaard, Jan. "A Study in the Chronology of op. 23–26 by Arnold Schoenberg." *Dansk Aarbog for Musikforskning* (1962), 93–115.

Stein, Erwin. "New Formal Principles." In *Orpheus in New Guises*, pp. 57–77. London, 1953.

Discography

The Complete Music for Solo Piano. Glenn Gould, piano. Columbia MS 7098 (1968).

Schönberg: Intégrale de l'oeuvre pour piano. Claude Helffer, piano. Harmonia mundi HM 252 (1968).

Jürg von Vintschger, piano. Turnabout TV-S 34378 (1970).

Arnold Schoenberg Piano Music. Paul Jacobs, piano. Nonesuch H 71309 (1975).

Arnold Schoenberg: The Piano Music. Maurizio Pollini, piano. Deutsche Grammophon 2530531 (1975).

Die Klaviermusik der neue wiener Schule. Yuji Takahaskhi, piano. Denon OX 7159–7160 (1979).

© 1923, renewed 1951, by Edition Wilhelm Hansen, Copenhagen.

sf
15
cresc
p
dolce
sf
sfp
pp
poco pes..
tempo
f
f
poco rit
p.
ff
3
20
dolce
p
legato (ohne Pedal!)

rit
poco rit
tempo
25
poco accel
dolce
tempo
sfp
30
(ohne Pedal!)

◆7◆

Henry Cowell (1897–1965)

The Banshee *(1925)*

The Banshee is one of several pictures in sound composed by Henry Cowell in the early decades of the twentieth century that develop new methods of playing the piano. Beginning with "The Tides of Manaunaun" in 1912, Cowell exploited tone clusters to create harmonies made from major and minor seconds. In 1923 he experimented with composition for "string piano," in which the player directly manipulates the strings inside of the instrument. Each of these studies relies upon sound to convey an image suggested by its title.

The Banshee, for string piano, evokes the mournful wail of this creature from Irish myth. According to Gaelic legend, the banshee was an ancestor from the realm of death who returned to the family to claim another soul. Its presence was announced by its unearthly shriek.

Bibliography

Music of the Twentieth Century, Chapter 11.

Discography

Piano Music of Henry Cowell. Henry Cowell, piano. Circle CWS 3 (1951) (including a supplementary record on which the composer discusses the music).

Sounds of New Music. Henry Cowell, piano. Folkways FX 6160 (1958).

Piano Music of Henry Cowell. Henry Cowell, piano. Folkways Records FM 3349 (1963).

Sound Forms for Piano. Robert Miller, piano. New World 203 (1976).

The Piano Music of Henry Cowell. Doris Hays, piano. Finnadar FIN 9016 (1977).

Explanation of Symbols

"The Banshee" is played on the open strings of the piano, the player standing at the crook. Another person must sit at the keyboard and hold down the damper pedal throughout the composition. The whole work should be played an octave lower than written.

R. H. stands for "right hand." L. H. stands for "left hand." Different ways of playing the strings are indicated by a letter over each tone, as follows:

(A) indicates a sweep with the flesh of the finger from the lowest string up to the note given.

(B) sweep lengthwise along the string of the note given with flesh of finger.

(C) sweep up and back from lowest A to highest B-flat given in this composition.

(D) pluck string with flesh of finger, where written, instead of octave lower.

(E) sweep along three notes together, in the same manner as (B).

(F) sweep in the manner of (B) but with the back of finger-nail instead of flesh.

(G) when the finger is half way along the string in the manner of (F), start a sweep along the same string with the flesh of the other finger, thus partly damping the sound.

(H) sweep back and forth in the manner of (C), but start at the same time from both above and below, crossing the sweep in the middle.

(I) sweep along five notes, in the manner of (B).

(J) same as (I) but with back of finger-nails instead of flesh of finger.

(K) sweep along in manner of (J) with nails of both hands together, taking in all notes between the two outer limits given.

(L) sweep in manner of (C) with flat of hand instead of single finger.

Copyright © 1930 by W. A. Quincke and Company. Used by arrangement with Associated Music Publishers, Inc.

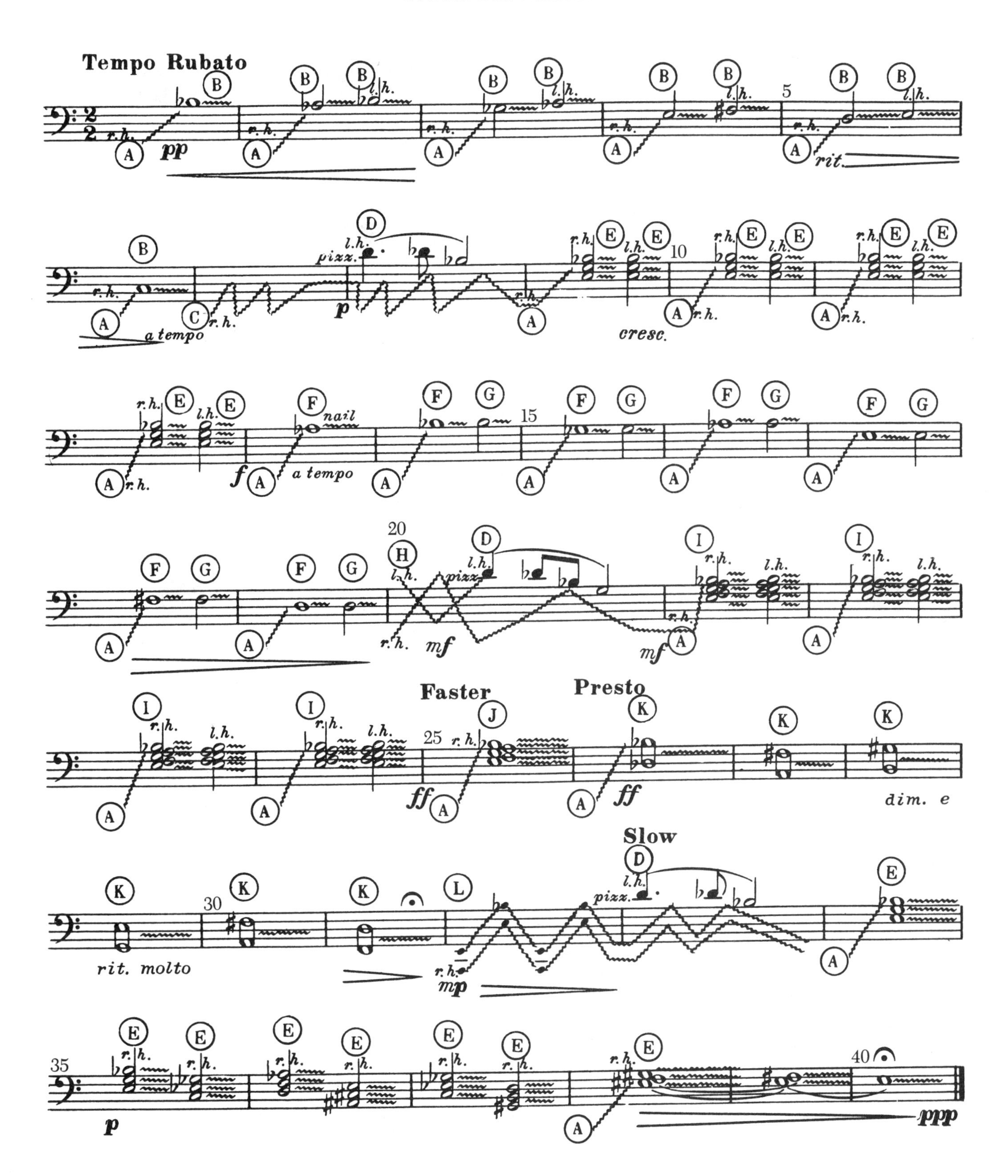
Tempo Rubato
r.h.
l.h.
pp
rit.
pizz.
a tempo
cresc.
nail
f
mf
Faster
Presto
ff
dim. e
Slow
rit. molto
mp
p
ppp

8

Sergei Prokofiev (1891–1953)

Seventh Piano Sonata (1939–42): Third Movement (finale)

Prokofiev sketched his Seventh Piano Sonata in 1939 and completed it in 1942, during a period when he had been evacuated from Moscow in the face of advancing German forces. The work was first heard upon his return to Moscow in 1943. Sviatoslav Richter, who played the premier performance, interprets the progressive style of the piece as an expression of wartime anxiety:

> The sonata immediately throws one into the anxious situation of the world losing its equilibrium. Anxiety and uncertainty reign. Man is witnessing the riot of the violent forces of death and destruction.

The Seventh Sonata is indeed one of Prokofiev's most dissonant and chromatic works. The finale is a perpetuum mobile in which Prokofiev's customary lyricism gives way to driving asymmetrical rhythms.

Bibliography

Music of the Twentieth Century, Chapter 8.

Richter, Sviatoslav. "On Prokofiev." In *Sergei Prokofiev: Materials, Articles, Interviews*, pp. 182–98. [Moscow], 1978.

Discography

Maurizio Pollini, piano. Deutsche Grammophon 2530225 (1972).

Vladimir Ashkenazy, piano. London CS 6573 (1969).

The Horowitz Collection. Vladimir Horowitz, piano. RCA Red Seal ARM1 2952 (1978, recorded in 1945); ARK1 2952 (cassette tape).

Paul Rutman Plays Russian Piano Works. Paul Rutman, piano. Odyssey Y 34634 (1978).

Richter Plays Russian Piano Music. Sviatoslav Richter, piano. Musical Heritage Society MHS 7036 (1979).

A (mm. 1-50)
Precipitato
mp
5
10
mf
15
cresc.
20
f
mf

25
30
35
40
f

45
cresc.
ff
p
50
mf
f marcato
55
60
f marcato

65
f
f marcato
70
75
p
f
80
mf non legato

mf espress.
85
p
90
p
mp
cresc.
95
f
non legato
100
8

8
105
dètachè
f marcato
110
f
115
f marcato
120

125
ff
mp
130
cresc.
135
140

145
f
m.d.
150
f
8
155
160

165
170
ff detaché
8
175
ff
8

9

John Cage (1912-   )

Two Pieces for Piano:

Sonatas and Interludes (1946–48): Sonata no. 5
Music of Changes *(1951): movement 4, section 1*

Sonatas and Interludes—a cycle of sixteen sonatas and four interludes—is Cage's longest and most substantial work for prepared piano, a medium that he began to explore in the late 1930s. In music of this type, the sound of the piano is transformed by mutes placed between the strings of certain notes. Within each piece in this cycle of works, the pitches and other sounds are intuitively selected—"chosen as one chooses shells while walking along a beach," the composer writes. The form of the sonatas, which is independent of their content of sounds and pitches, consists of durational patterns in which the lengths of subsections create simple numerical ratios with one another. In Sonata no. 5, for example, the binary form is divided (by double bars) into sections whose total number of half-note values is 18/18/18/18/9, that is, 2/2/2/2/1. It is necessary for this sonata to be studied in connection with a recording, since the preparation of the instrument produces sounds that deviate from their notated appearance.

Music of Changes is written for conventional piano. It consists of four large movements, each in numerous sections. The form—like that of Cage's Sonatas and Interludes—is determined by a succession of durations. But the configuration of pitches and rests that fills these durational spans is chosen by procedures of chance, thus banishing—at least in part—the composer's taste and intuition. The work becomes, in Cage's words, "an activity characterized by process [which is] essentially purposeless."

Cage's chance procedures require many notational peculiarities. Each measure contains four beats at the metronomic speed shown above the staff. But the performer cannot rely upon traditional counting. Instead, a note or figure begins at the point at which it is notated from left to right in the measure. For example, a note placed midway in the measure is to be played when half of the time devoted to that measure has elapsed. The fractions above and below groups of notes or rests tell which part of the beat is occupied by that figure or rest. A cross is placed at the point in a measure at which a sustained note or pedal is to be released.

Bibliography

Music of the Twentieth Century, Chapters 11 and 13.

Cage, John. "Changes" and "To Describe the Process of Composition Used in *Music of Changes* and *Imaginary Landscape* no. 4." In *Silence,* pp. 18–34 and 57–59. Middletown, Conn., 1961.

Griffiths, Paul. *Cage.* Oxford Studies of Composers (18), pp. 19–29. London, New York, Melbourne, 1981.

Discography

(Sonata no. 5). Maro Ajemian, piano. Dial 19–20 (1951); reissued, Composers Recordings CRI 199 (ca. 1965).

Sound Forms for Piano. Robert Miller, piano. New World W 203 (1976).

Joshua Pierce, piano. Tomato Records TOM 2 1001 (1977).

Contemporary Piano Music. Klára Kormendi, piano. Hungaroton SLPX 12569 (1985).

(*Music of Changes,* movements 3–4). David Tudor, piano. New World NW 214 (1978).

Sonata no. 5

TONE	MATERIAL	STRINGS LEFT TO RIGHT	DISTANCE FROM DAMPER (INCHES)	MATERIAL	STRINGS LEFT TO RIGHT	DISTANCE FROM DAMPER (INCHES)	MATERIAL	STRINGS LEFT TO RIGHT	DISTANCE FROM DAMPER (INCHES)	TONE
16va				SCREW	2-3	1 1/4*				A
				MED. BOLT	2-3	1 3/8*				G
				SCREW	2-3	1 5/8*				F
				SCREW	2-3	1 13/16*				E
				SCREW	2-3	1 3/4*				E♭
				SM. BOLT	2-3	2*				D
				SCREW	2-3	1 11/16*				C♯
				FURNITURE BOLT	2-3	2 3/16*				C
				SCREW	2-3	2 1/2*				B
				SCREW	2-3	1 7/8*				B♭
				MED. BOLT	2-3	2 7/8*				A
				SCREW	2-3	2 1/4*				A♭
				SCREW	2-3	3 3/4*				G
				SCREW	2-3	2 5/16*				F♯
	SCREW	1-2	3/4*	FURN. BOLT + 2 NUTS	2-3	2 1/8*	SCREW + 2 NUTS	2-3	3 1/4*	F
				SCREW	2-3	1 13/16*				E
				FURNITURE BOLT	2-3	1 7/8				E♭
				SCREW	2-3	1 15/16				C♯
				SCREW	2-3	1 1/16				C
8va	(DAMPER TO BRIDGE = 4 [illegible]; ADJUST ACCORDINGLY)			MED. BOLT	2-3	3 3/[illegible]				B
				SCREW	2-3	4 7/16				A
	RUBBER	1-2-3	4 1/2	FURNITURE BOLT	2-3	1 1/4				G♯
				SCREW	2-3	1 3/4				F♯
				SCREW	2-3	2 5/16				F
	RUBBER	1-2-3	5 3/4							E
	RUBBER	1-2-3	0 1/2	FURN. BOLT + NUT	2-3	0 7/8				E♭
				FURNITURE BOLT	2-3	2 1/16				D
	RUBBER	1-2-3	3 5/8							D♭
				BOLT	2-3	7 1/8				C
				BOLT	2-3	2				B
	SCREW	1-2	10	SCREW	2-3	1	RUBBER	1-2-3	8 1/4	B♭
	(PLASTIC (OVER D))	1-2-3	2 15/16				RUBBER	1-2-3	4 1/2	G♯
	PLASTIC (OVER 1 UNDER 2-3)	1-2-3	2 7/8				RUBBER	1-2-3	10 1/8	G
	(PLASTIC (OVER D))	1-2-3	4 1/4				RUBBER	1-2-3	5 7/16	F♯
	PLASTIC (OVER 1 UNDER 2-3)	1-2-3	4 1/8				RUBBER	1-2-3	9 3/4	D
	BOLT	1-2	15 1/2	BOLT	2-3	11/16	RUBBER	1-2-3	14 1/8	D♭
	BOLT	1-2	4 1/2	BOLT	2-3	7/8	RUBBER	1-2-3	0 1/2	C
	BOLT	1-2	4 3/4	BOLT	2-3	1/16	RUBBER	1-2-3	[illegible]	B
	RUBBER	1-2-3	4 1/2	MED. BOLT	2-3	10 1/8				B♭
	SCREW	1-2	5 7/8	LG. BOLT	2-3	5 7/8	SCREW + NUTS	1-2	1	A
	BOLT	1-2	7 1/8	MED. BOLT	2-3	2 1/4	RUBBER	1-2-3	4 1/8	A♭
	LONG BOLT	1-2	8 3/4	LG. BOLT	2-3	3 1/4				G
				BOLT	2-3	11/16				D
8va bassa	SCREW + RUBBER	1-2	4 7/16							D
16va bassa	ERASER (OVER D UNDER C♯ + E♭) AM. PENCIL CO. #346	1	6 3/4							D

*MEASURE FROM BRIDGE.

Reprinted by permission of C. F. Peters Corporation.

(4 beats)
2
+
(4 beats)
2
+
5
2 1/2
(5 beats)
+
(5 beats)
2 1/2
10
15
20
25
30
35
40

Music of Changes

Reprinted by permission of C. F. Peters Corporation.

15
104
PIZZ.
PIZZ.
PIZZ.
(NORMAL)
ARP.-GLISS.
ON STRINGS
(FINGERNAIL)
20
BOTH
ARMS
(sustenuto
pedal)

104
ACCEL.
FOREARM-ARPEGG.
SCRATCH STRINGS
LENGTHWISE;
(FINGERNAILS)
ARP.-GLISS. ON STRINGS
FINGERTIPS; BEYOND DAMPERS
25
(R.H.)
L.H.
108
ACCEL.
30

10

Gabriel Fauré (1845–1924)

"Dans la forêt de septembre," op. 85, no. 1 (1902)

The *mélodies* of Fauré wed the depth of expression of German lieder to the traditional color of French music and to the restraint and fluidity of nineteenth-century French poetry. The text of "Dans la forêt de septembre" is by Catulle Mendès (1841–1909), one of the founders of the Parnassian school of poetry. The Parnassians sought an elegant perfection of poetic form and language and espoused a lofty aestheticism. Fauré treats the six stanzas of Mendès's poem as a rondo: music of the first stanza is repeated in a varied shape in the third stanza and again near the end of the song, beginning with the last line of the fifth stanza.

TEXT

In September's Forest

Weakened, murmuring branches,
Sonorous tree trunks, hollowed by age,
The ancient, aching forest
Is in tune with our melancholy.

O fir trees clinging to the gorge,
Dry nests in broken boughs,
Burnt thickets, flowers without dew,
You know of suffering!

And when man, entering palely,
Cries in your solitary woods,
Shadowy and mysterious plaints
Greet him with sympathetic tears.

Good forest! Open promise
Of the exile which life implores,
I come with footsteps still quick
Into your depths still green.

But from a slender birch on the path,
A russet leaf grazes
My head and lights trembling on my shoulder.

The aging forest—
Knowing that winter where all miscarries
is now at hand in me as in it—
Presents me with a fraternal tribute
Of its first dead leaf!

Bibliography

Music of the Twentieth Century, Chapter 8.

Meister, Barbara. *Nineteenth-Century French Song: Fauré, Chausson, Duparc, and Debussy*, pp. 117–20. Bloomington, 1980.

Noske, Frits. *French Song from Berlioz to Duparc*, pp. 255–72. 2d ed., rev. Rita Benton and Frits Noske, trans. Rita Benton. New York, 1970.

Discography

Gérard Souzay, baritone; Dalton Baldwin, piano. Philips 835286AY (1969).

Bernard Kruysen, baritone; Noël Lee, piano. Telefunken SAT 22546 (1973).

Mélodies complètes. Jacques Herbillon, baritone; Théodore Paraskivesco, piano. Musical Heritage Society MHS 3438-3443 (1974).

Paris; Hamelle, 1902.

Nids dé-serts aux bran-ches bri - sé - - es, Hal-liers brû-
15
mf
- lés, fleurs sans ro - sé - - - - es,
mf
p
Vous savez bien com-me l'on souf - - fre!
dolce
Et lors - que
p
pp
20
3
l'homme, pas-sant blê - me, Pleu - re dans le bois so - li - tai - re, Des

25
plain-tes d'om-bre et de mys - tè - re L'ac-cueil-lent en pleu-rant dc
p
mê - me.
p
Bon-ne fo-rêt! pro-mes - se ou-
p dolce
30
- ver - te de l'e-xil que la vi-e im-plo - re, Je
viens d'un pas a-ler - te en - co - re Dans ta pro-fon -
3 poco cresc.

35
dolce
- deur en - cor ver - - te.
Mais d'un fin bou -
p dolce
- leau de la sen - - te, U - ne feuil - le,un peu rous - se, frô - le Ma
40
tê - te et trem - ble à mon é - pau - le;
espressivo
cresc.
f
p
C'est que la fo-rêt vieil-lis - san - te, Sa -
p dolce

45
-chant l'hi-ver, où tout a - vor - te, Dé-jà pro-che en moi comme en
el - - le, Me fait l'au-mô - - ne fra-ter-
f
f
50
-nel - le De sa pre - miè - re feuil - le
p
p
mor - - te!

• 11 •

Alban Berg (1885–1935)

Four Songs, *op. 2 (ca. 1908–ca. 1910): "Warm die Lüfte"*

The four songs of Berg's opus 2 constitute a cycle unified by poetic images of sleep and dreams and by recurrent musical elements. These pieces are transitional in style between Berg's earlier romantic manner and his later atonal language. Indeed, the last song, "Warm die Lüfte," is his first completely atonal work.

The conclusion of this song from measure 20 recapitulates harmonic materials from earlier pieces of the cycle, especially from the first song. The pessimism expressed by the words of this passage may reflect Berg's own despair at the difficulties of his courtship with his future wife, Helene Nahowski. The first edition of the cycle (1910) was dedicated to Fräulein Nahowski, but this gesture is absent in the revised version of the songs which was published in 1928.

The passage in "Warm die Lüfte" from measures 20 and 21, whose harmonies alternate between forms of all-interval tetrachords, was later duplicated by Claude Debussy in the fourth *Épigraphe antique* (m. 29–32).

TEXT

Warm is the air; grass sprouts on sunny meadows. Listen! Listen! The nightingale is piping. I shall sing. High above in the mountain's dusky woods, the cold snows are melting and glistening. A girl in somber dress leans upon a moist oak; sickly are her delicate cheeks. Her gray eyes burn feverishly among the gloomy giant trees. "He still has not come. He has abandoned me. . . ." Die! One dies while another lives: this makes the world so profoundly beautiful.

(from *Der Glühende* by Alfred Mombert)

Bibliography

Music of the Twentieth Century, Chapter 7.

Carner, Mosco. *Alban Berg: The Man and the Work*, pp. 98–101. 2d, rev. ed. New York, 1983.

Jarman, Douglas. *The Music of Alban Berg*, passim. Berkeley, 1979.

Redlich, Hans. *Alban Berg*, pp. 35–44. London, 1957.

Stuckenschmidt, H. H. "Debussy or Berg? The Mystery of a Chord Progression." *Musical Quarterly*, 51 (1965), 453–59.

Wennerstrom, Mary. "Pitch Relationships in Berg's Songs, op. 2." *Indiana Theory Review*, 1 (1977), 12–22.

Discography

Landmarks of 20th-Century Music. Heather Harper, soprano. Angel S 36480 (1968).

Songs of the New Vienna School. Dietrich Fischer-Dieskau, baritone. Deutsche Grammophon 2530107 (1972).

Frühe Lieder von Berg, Schönberg und Schreker. Elisabeth Speiser, voice; Irwin Gage, piano. Jecklin-Disko 561 (1982).

*Play the grace note quietly and slowly.

Berlin: Schlesinger'sche Buch- u. Musikhandlung, 1910.

accel.
rit.
Eich-stamm, krank sind ih - re zar - ten Wan - gen, die grau-en Au-gen fie - bern durch
15
accel.
rit.
Dü - ster - rie - sen - stäm - me.
„Er kommt noch nicht.
gliss.
Rit.
Accel.
molto
sffz
molto
gliss.
Coda (20-25)
fff
Er läßt mich war - ten..."
(tonlos)
Stirb!
20
p
Der Ei - ne
Rit.
Accel.
molto
sffz
Rit.
Accel.
ff martellato
l.H.
r.H.
molto rit.
ganz langsam
fff
p dolce
sffz
sehr ruhig
kurzer Halt.
25
stirbt, da - ne - ben der An - dre lebt:
Das macht die Welt so tief - schön.
espress.
mp
p
pp
ppp
all interval tetrachord

• 12 •

Charles Ives (1874–1954)

114 Songs:

"Charlie Rutlage" (1920–21)
"From Paracelsus*" (1921)*

In 1922 Charles Ives assembled a collection of *114 Songs* from among his works in this genre composed during the preceding three decades. The collection was published at his expense and distributed free of charge to musicians whom he thought might be interested in it. The songs are remarkably diverse in style and content. Their words are alternately philosophical statements, patriotic expressions, folk ballads, college songs, and texts used by nineteenth-century European song composers. In style the music alternates or intermingles the traditional and experimental: marches, folk-like tunes, sentimental ballads, and hymn tunes are juxtaposed with atonal music, semi-improvisatory pieces, and dissonant studies.

In the "Postface" to *114 Songs,* Ives asserts the philosophy behind the eclectic diversity of the collection and behind his own aspirations as a composer. Art, he says, is not elitist or self-reflective. It stems instead from the instincts of the common man and it celebrates everyday activities—one's work, the nation, ethical concerns, and family life.

"Charlie Rutlage" sets a cowboy ballad written by D. J. O'Malley. The song begins and ends in a folk-song style; the middle part is a dramatic recitation whose accompaniment ends in tone clusters hammered out by the fists of the pianist. "From *Paracelsus"* takes its words from a closet drama of Robert Browning. The music is a reworking of passages from Ives's *Robert Browning* Overture (1912).

Bibliography

Music of the Twentieth Century, Chapter 11.

Hitchcock, H. Wiley. "Charles Ives's Book of 114 Songs." *A Musical Offering: Essays in Honor of Martin Bernstein,* pp. 127–36. Ed. Claire Brook and E. H. Clinkscale. New York, 1977.

Ives, Charles E. Postface to *114 Songs.* In *Essays Before a Sonata, The Majority, and Other Writings,* pp. 120–31. Ed. Howard Boatwright. New York, 1962.

Discography

("Charlie Rutlage"). Marni Nixon, soprano; John McCabe, piano. Nonesuch H 71209 (1968).

American Scenes, American Portraits. Evelyn Lear, soprano; Thomas Stewart, baritone; Alan Mandel, piano. Columbia M 30229 (1971).

Roberta Alexander, voice; Tan Crone, piano. Etcetera KTC-1020 (compact disc, 1984).

("From *Paracelsus*"). The Art Song in America. John Kennedy Hanks, tenor; Ruth Friedberg, piano. Duke University Press (1965).

Ted Puffer, tenor; James Tenney, piano. Folkways Records FM 3344 (1966).

Jan DeGaetani, mezzo-soprano; Gilbert Kalish, piano. Nonesuch H 71325 (1976).

"Charlie Rutlage"

Used by arrangement with Associated Music Publishers, Inc.

"Charlie Rutlage" is predominantly a tonal and diatonic song w/ an atonal middle section.

* variation of the opening pentatonic melody.

free from earth-ly ills; But when it came to fin-ish up the
30
(a little slower)
(fast again)
work on which he went, Noth-ing came back from him; his time on earth was spent. 'Twas
(a little slower)
(fast again)
ff
as he rode the round up, a XIT turned back to the herd; Poor Char-lie shoved him in a-gain, his
35
faster and faster - - - louder and louder
faster and faster - - - fff louder and louder
cut-ting horse he spurred; An - oth-er turned; at that moment his
fff

(CLIMAX)
40
mp slower
p
horse the creature spied and turned and fell with him, beneath poor Charlie died, His
ffff
mp loco
C, D, E, G, A (pentatonic)
*fists
8va lower
r.h.
l.h.
slower
p
Return to Beginning Music
(Tone Clusters)
as in the beginning
F, D#, C#, B, A#, G# (Pentatonic Superset)
45
D, E, F#, A, B (pent.)
relations in Texas his face never more will see, But I hope he'll meet his loved ones beyond in eterni-ty, in
about the time at the beginning
(folk-song style)
eternity, I hope he'll meet his parents, will meet them face to face, And that they'll
mf
50
pp
grasp him by the right hand at the shining throne, the shin - ing throne, the shining throne of grace.
*In these measures, the notes are indicated only approximately; the time of course, is the main point.
Bb: V7 I V7 I IV I
(plagal cadence)

(1921)

"From *Paracelsus*" (Robert Browning)

music is reworking of passages from Ives' Robert Browning Overture (1912)

Allegro

with marked energy

animando

For God is glo-ri-fied in man, And to man's

(Notes not marked otherwise, are natural)

General Form: loud to soft, intense to calm, complex to simple

© 1935 Merion Music Inc. Used by permission of the publisher.

he is first devoted to power (mm. 1–15)

10
mf with less energy
glo - ry vowed I soul and limb. Yet, con-sti-tu-ted thus, and thus endowed, I failed:
l.h.
l.h.
(nearly-whole-tone hexachords)
(high descant)
mf
parallel 5th's
3
B minor triad
(tone cluster)
pentatonic sets
ff I gazed on power, I gazed on
con moto giusto
f
ref. oct.
ff
power till I grew blind........
p
mp slower
What wonder if I saw no way to shun despair? The
l.h. l.h. l.h. l.h.
mp
tr
pp
slower
whole-tone chords
Tone cluster

* m. 15 — chords in piano held through each other w/ damper pedal.

15

Simple tonal, Vocal melody (Key of G)

Andante molto

mf *p*

power I sought seemed God's.................... .... I learned my own deep er - ror, And

mf no counterpoint! (Wedge Figure)

maestoso (bitriadic harmonies) *p* (G)

Ped. ....

He perceives its (power's) limitations (mm. 16–17)

except for a few chromatic ornaments, vocal melody stays in G.

p

what pro-por-tion love should hold with power in man's right con-sti - tu-tion; Al - ways pre-

non cresc.

(whole-tone chords)

* The strands of the music come gently together

20

open D chord

p

ce-ding power, * And with much power, ——— al - ways, al - ways much more love;....

p

He finally understands that power must be preceeded by love! (mm. 17–20)

• 13 •

Paul Hindemith (1895–1963)

Das Marienleben *(1923): "Vom Tode Mariä I"*

Paul Hindemith's song cycle *Das Marienleben (The Life of Mary)* marks the end of his youthful period of musical experimentation and the beginning of a neoclassical orientation which he steadfastly pursued from this time. Hindemith's music in the fifteen songs of this monumental collection is objective and coolly detached from the emotions of the text; the texture is predominantly contrapuntal, there is regularity of rhythm and meter, and traditional forms are employed.

The texts of *Das Marienleben* are a cycle of lengthy poems in prose by Rainer Maria Rilke (1875–1926) describing events in the life of the Blessed Virgin Mary. The collection is concluded by three poems "On the Death of Mary." The first of these tells of Mary's last days on earth. Hindemith's setting is in a ternary form, whose outer sections are variations upon a five-measure ground bass. As an expression of Mary's dignity and majesty, the music is a severe polyphonic invention stripped of all extraneous details.

In 1948 Hindemith completed a revision of the cycle in which most of the songs were made more regular in phrasing and harmony.

TEXT

The same great angel which had earlier brought her tidings of her conception, stood there, waiting until she noticed him. And he spoke, "It is now time that you appear." And she was frightened as before and, humbly acquiescing, became again as the maiden. Then he became radiant and, nearing her infinitely, vanished as into her face. And he called together the widely dispersed Disciples to the house on the slope, the house of the Last Supper. They came gravely and entered fearfully. There she lay, along the narrow bedstead, mysteriously immersed in her end and in her chosen state—entirely unharmed, as one unused, listening to the song of angels. Now when she saw them waiting behind their candles, she tore herself from the abundance of voices and, with a full heart, gave away the two robes which she owned. And she raised up her countenance to this one and that one. . . . (O source of nameless streams of tears.) Then she sank back in weakness and drew the heavens so near to Jerusalem that her soul, setting forth, had only to stretch itself a little, for He who knew everything about her was even then raising her to her godly nature.

Bibliography

Music of the Twentieth Century, Chapter 10.

Kemp, Ian. *Hindemith*. Oxford Studies of Composers (6), pp. 13–14. London, Oxford, 1970.

Skelton, Geoffrey. *Paul Hindemith: The Man Behind the Music*, pp. 75–77. New York, 1975.

Truscott, Harold. "Hindemith and *Das Marienleben*." *Musical Times*, 110 (1969), 1240–42.

Discography

Paul Hindemith Anthology, Vol. 7. Peggy Bonini, soprano; Ingolf Dahl, piano. GSC Recordings 7 (1977).

Roxolana Roslak, soprano; Glenn Gould, piano. Columbia M2 34597 (1978).

E♭ D♭ A♭ B♭ F G C D♮ A♮

G A♭ (A♮) B♭ C D♭ D E♭ F G

© B. Schott's Soehne, Mainz 1924. © renewed. All rights reserved. Used by permission of European American Music Distributors Corporation, sole U.S. agent for B. Schott's Soehne.

10
p
mp
ſprach: Jetzt wird es Zeit, daß du er - ſcheinſt. Und ſie er - ſchrak wie da - mals und er - wies ſich
p
pp sehr zart
mf
15
p
wie - - der als die Magd, ihn tief be - ja - hend. Er a - ber
mf
ſtrahl - - te, und un - end - lich na - - hend, ſchwand er wie in ihr An - ge -
p
20
ſicht, und hieß die weit - - hin aus - ge - gan - ge - nen Be - keh - - rer zu -

25
Noch lang-
mf
p
sam - men-kom-men in das Haus am Hang, das Haus des A - bendmahls.
the House of the Last Supper.
ritenuto
mf
p
pp
samer (♪=104-112)
pp sehr ruhig
Sie ka-men schwe-rer und tra - ten ban-ge ein: Da lag, ent-
l.H.
30
p
pp
lang die schma-le Bett-statt, die in Un - ter-gang und Aus-er-wäh -
mp
ruhig
35
p
- lung rät-sel-haft Ge-tauch - te, ganz un - ver-sehrt, wie ei-ne Un-ge-brauch-

pp
te, und ach - te - te auf eng - li - ſchen Ge -
pp
40
ſang. Nun da ſie al - le hin - ter ih - ren Ker - zen
p
ppp
pp
ab - war - ten ſah, riß ſie vom Ü - ber - maß der Stim - men
p
45
ſich und ſchenk - te noch von Her - zen die bei - den Klei - der fort, die ſie be - ſaß,
f
mp
poco f

mf
und hob ihr Antlitz auf___ zu dem und dem.... (O Ursprung na-men-lo-ser Trä- - - - - - - - - -nen-bä-che.)
50
p
mf
mp
pp
55
ritenuto
Wie zuerst
pp
Sie a-ber leg-te sich in ih-re Schwä- -che und zog die
60
Him- -mel an Je ru- - -sa-lem so nah her-an, daß ih-re
mp
p

65
mf
See - - le nur, aus-tre - tend, sich ein we-nig strecken muß - - te, schon hob
p
70
er sie, der al - - - - - - les von ihr wuß - te,
poco f
poco f
hin - - ein in ih - re gött - - - - -
mf
75
p
- - li - - che Na - tur.
molto riten.
p
mf
pp

• 14 •

Benjamin Britten (1913–76)

Serenade for Tenor, Horn and Strings, op. 31 (1943): "Dirge"

Britten composed the Serenade shortly after returning to England from his wartime sojourn in Canada and the United States. It was originally geared to the virtuosic skills of the tenor Peter Pears and hornist Dennis Brain. The cycle is begun by a soliloquy for valveless horn, which is repeated offstage at the conclusion. The six vocal movements are settings of poetic works by Charles Cotton (1630–87), Alfred, Lord Tennyson (1809–92), William Blake (1757–1827), Ben Jonson (ca. 1573–1637), John Keats (1795–1821) and of an anonymous fifteenth-century Scottish dirge.

The Dirge exemplifies Britten's reinterpretation of triadic tonality. The vocal line is an ostinato that repeatedly outlines a G-minor triad. The orchestral commentary, which takes the form of a fugue, is centered on a tonality of E♭.

Bibliography

Music of the Twentieth Century, Chapter 10.

Evans, Peter. *The Music of Benjamin Britten*, pp. 91–94. London, 1979.

Palmer, Christopher. "Embalmer of the Night: The Orchestral Song Cycles." In *The Britten Companion*, pp. 308–28. Ed. Christopher Palmer. Cambridge, 1984.

Discography

Peter Pears, tenor; Dennis Brain, horn; New Symphony Orchestra of London, Eugene Goossens, conductor. Decca-Eclipse ECS 507 (1969).

Peter Pears, tenor; Barry Tuckwell, horn; London Symphony Orchestra, Benjamin Britten, conductor. London 26161 (1971).

Robert Tear, tenor; Alan Civil, horn; Northern Sinfonia Orchestra, Neville Marriner, conductor. Angel-EMI SXLP 30194 (1971).

Peter Pears, tenor; Dennis Brain, horn; Boyd Neel String Orchestra, Benjamin Britten, conductor. Decca-Eclipse ECM 814 (1979, recorded in 1944).

Robert Tear, tenor; Dale Clevenger, horn; Chicago Symphony Orchestra, Carlo Maria Giulini, conductor. Deutsche Grammophon 2531199 (1979).

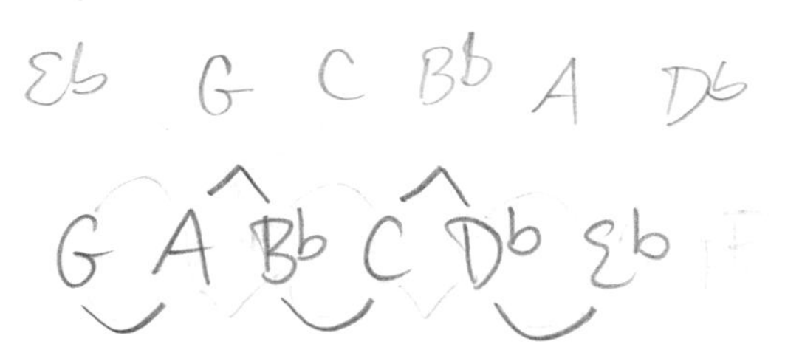

© Copyright 1944 in U.S.A. by Hawkes & Sons (London) Ltd. Copyright for all countries. Used by permission.

G, Ab, D, E, C#, Bb, Db, F#

G, Ab, Bb, C#, (Db), D, E, F#, G

Voice
Sit thee down and put them on;.......... And Christe re - ceive thy saule..... If
Hn. in F
Vln. I
Vln. II
cresc.
fp
cresc.
fp
Vla.
'Cello
Bass
4th vocal ent.
20
hos'n and shoon thou ne'er gav'st nane,
E-very nighte and alle, The
4th fugal ent. - D
mf marc.
cresc.

Voice
whinnes sall prick thee to the bare bane;........ And Christe re - ceive thy saule......... From
Hn. in F
episode (ms. 24-
Vln. I
fp
fp cresc.
f pesante
Vln. II
fp cresc.
f pesante
Vla.
fp cresc.
f pesante
'Cello
fp cresc.
f pesante
Bass
fp cresc.
f pesante
5th vocal ent.
DEVELOPMENTAL
25
Voice
Whin - ny - muir when thou may'st pass, E-ver-y nighte and alle, To
Hn. in F
Vln. I
sfp
Vln. II
sfp
Vla.
sfp
'Cello
Bass
f stacc. e pesante sempre

30
Voice
Hn. in F
Vln. I
Vln. II
Vla.
'Cello
Bass
Brig o' Dread thou com'st at last; .... And Christe re - ceive thy saule.... From
cresc.
sfp
f stacc. e pesante
pizz.
arco
6th vocal ent.
Brig o' Dread when thou may'st pass, E-ver-y nighte and alle, To
Fugue subj. in horn – E
(veloce)
molto f largamente
ffp
ff
f marc.
Tutti (everything lines-up)

35
Voice
Pur-ga-to-ry fire thou com'st at last; .... And Christe re - - ceive thy saule........ If
Hn. in F
ffp cresc.
ffp cresc.
ffp
Vln. I
Vln. II
Vla.
arco
f marc.
'Cello
Bass
f
7th vocal ent.
Voice
e - ver thou gav'st meat or drink, E-ver-y nighte and alle, The
Hn. in F
f marc. dim.
sempre più p
False entry (fragmentary) - A
Vln. I
p dim.
Vln. II
p
Vla.
dim.
mf
'Cello
dim.
mf
Bass
dim.
mf

40
Voice
fire sall ne-ver make thee shrink;.. And Christe re - ceive thy saule............... If
Hn. in F
pp
Key change
Vln. I
pp
Bb
Vln. II
pp
D
Vla.
p
E
pp
'Cello
p
pizz.
pp
C
Bass
p
pp
STRETTO (HEAD OF SUBJ.)
8th vocal ent.
45
Voice
meat or drink thou ne'er gav'st nane, E-ver-y nighte and alle, The
Hn. in F
Vln. I
fpp
Vln. II
fpp
Vla.
fpp
'Cello
arco
pp
fpp
Bass

9th (final) vocal ent.
(same text as beg.)
Voice
Hn. in F
Vln. I
Vln. II
Vla.
'Cello
Bass
fire will burn thee to the bare bane;.... And Christe re - ceive thy saule................. This ae nighte,
div.
fpp
pp dim.
pp
p distinto
50
senza ritardando
this ae nighte, E-ver-y nighte and alle, Fire and fleet and candle-lighte, And Christe re-ceive thy saule....
unis.
pizz.
ppp
meno f ma sempre distinto
dim.
Fragment (Head) — Eb

•15•

Pierre Boulez (1925-)

Le marteau sans maître *(1954, revised 1957): "L'artisanat furieux"*

Boulez's *Le marteau sans maître (The Hammer Without Master)* is one of a number of works by European composers of the 1950s which explore new ways of setting a text by assimilating poetic structures into musical syntax. Boulez selects three surrealistic poems by René Char which he sets to music for voice and differing chamber ensembles. The sections with text are elaborated by instrumental movements which function as commentaries, preludes, or epilogues. Boulez calls upon the alto voice to sing in different manners, including Schoenbergian speaking voice, vocalization, singing with the mouth closed, and a virtuosic style requiring instrumental agility. All of these contribute to a subtle expression of both the meaning and structure of the words.

The third movement, "L'artisanat furieux," is indebted in its medium of voice and flute to the seventh movement of Schoenberg's *Pierrot lunaire.* The music maintains great freedom from regular beat or rhythm and from traditional textures. The structures of pitch are systematically chosen according to Boulez's method of "multiplication of frequencies" (an explanation of which is found in the article by Lev Koblyakov cited below).

TEXT

The Raging Proletariat

The red caravan at the perimeter of the jail
And a corpse in the basket
And work horses in the horseshoe
I dream of my head on the tip of my Peruvian knife

Bibliography

Music of the Twentieth Century, Chapter 12.

Griffiths, Paul. *Boulez.* Oxford Studies of Composers (16), pp. 28–38. London, New York, Melbourne, 1978.

Koblyakov, Lev. "Pierre Boulez, *Le marteau sans maître:* Analysis of Pitch Structure." *Zeitschrift für Musiktheorie*, 8 (1977), 24–39.

Stockhausen, Karlheinz. "Music and Speech." *Die Reihe*, 6 (1960, English trans. 1964), 40–64.

Discography

Jeanne Deroubaix, alto; Pierre Boulez, conductor. Turnabout 34081S (1966).

Music of Our Time. Robert Craft, conductor. Odyssey 32160154 (1968).

Boulez Conducts Boulez. Yvonne Minton, mezzo-soprano; Ensemble Musique Vivante. Columbia M 32160 (1973).

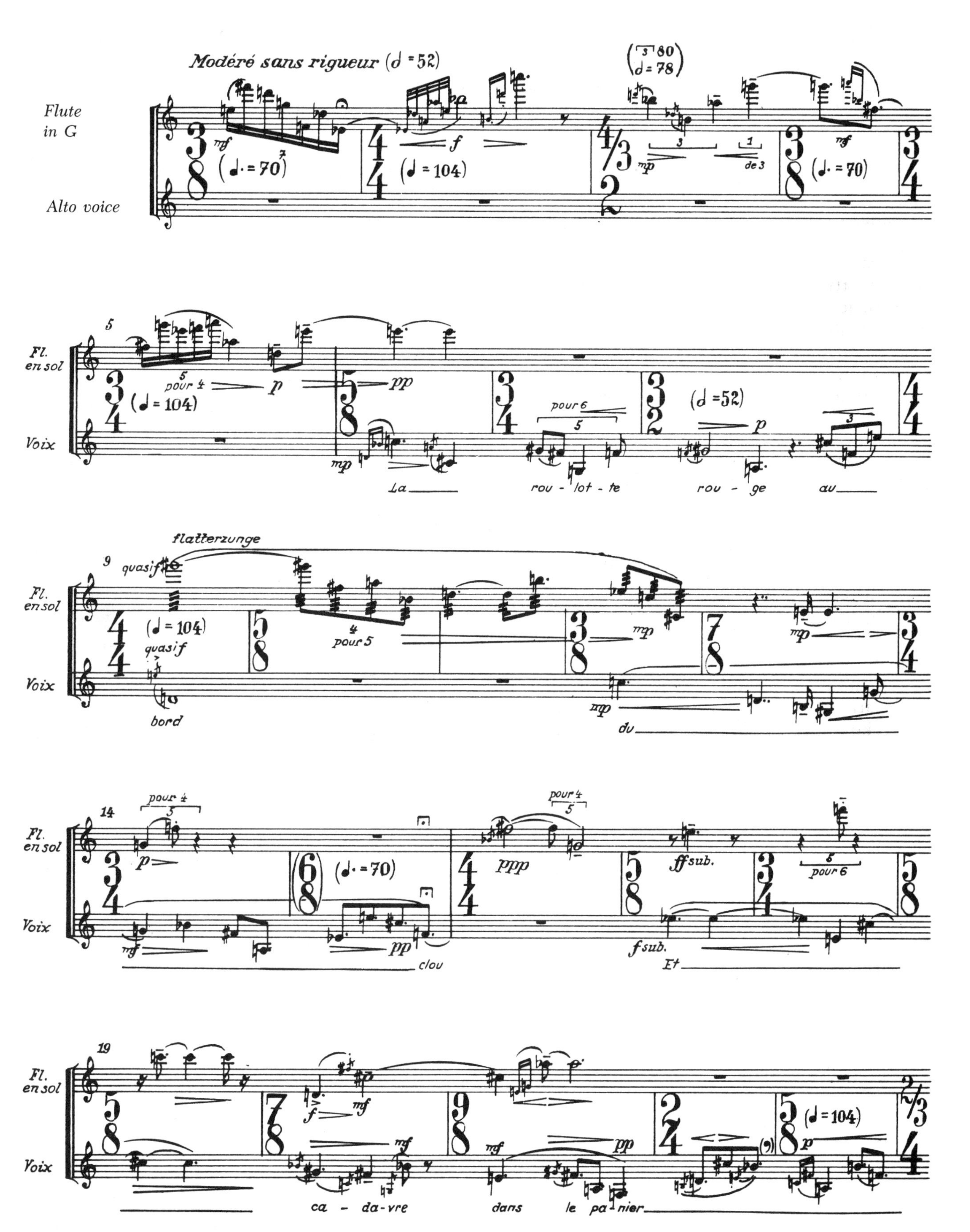

© Copyright 1954 by Universal Edition (London) Ltd., London. All rights reserved. Used by permission of European American Music Distributors Corporation, sole U.S. agent for Universal Edition.

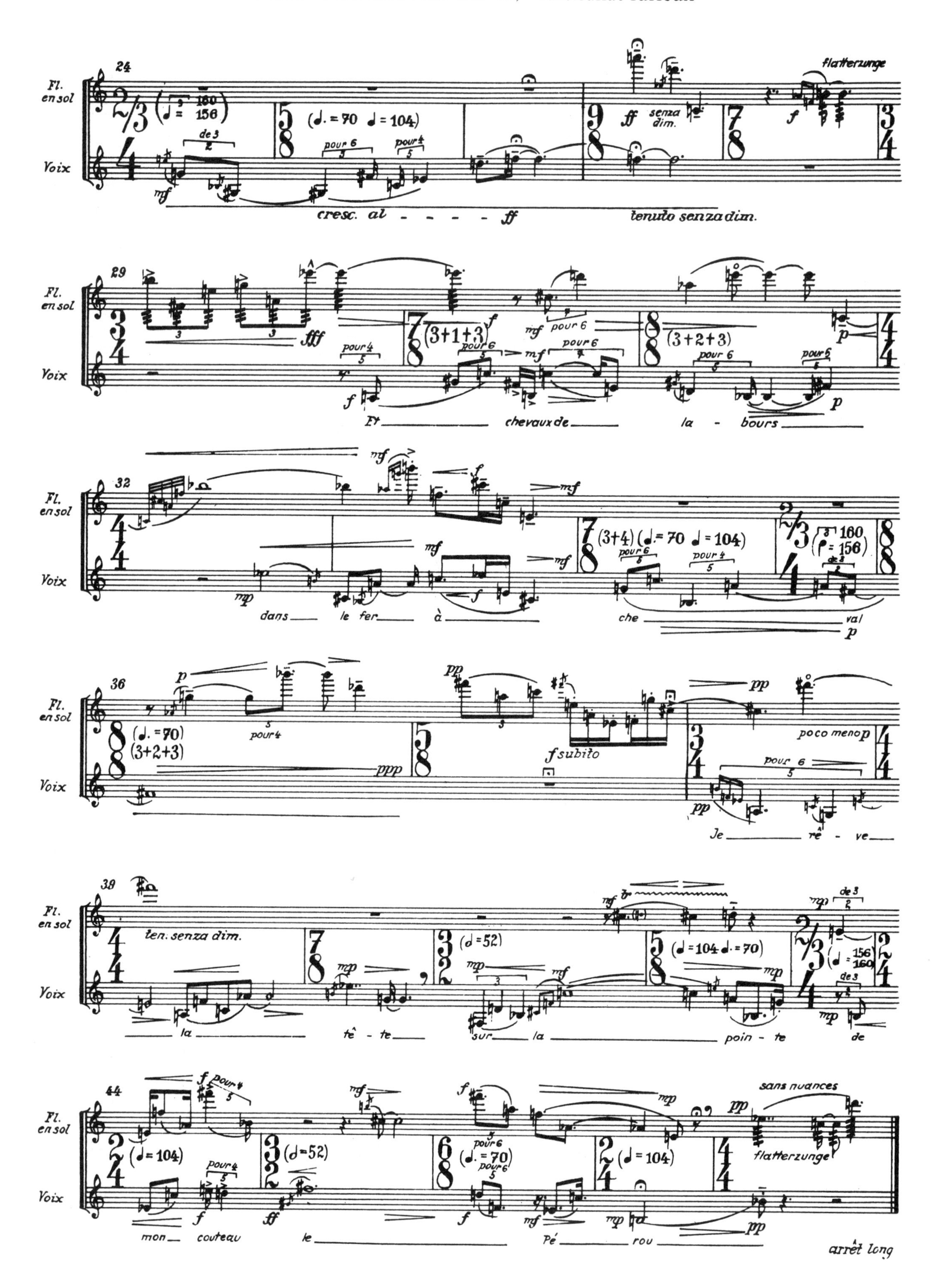
Fl. en sol
Voix
flatterzunge
senza dim.
cresc. al
tenuto senza dim.
Et
chevaux de
la - bours
dans
le fer
à
che
val
f subito
poco meno p
Je
rê - ve
ten. senza dim.
la
tê - te
sur
la
poin - te
de
sans nuances
flatterzunge
mon
couteau
le
Pé
rou
arrêt long

• 16 •

Luciano Berio (1925–)

Folk Songs *(1964):*
"Black Is the Color of My True Love's Hair"

The genre of the folk-song arrangement enjoyed great popularity in the first half of the twentieth century in works of Bartók, Milhaud, Ravel, Falla, Ives, Britten, and Vaughan Williams. Although it lost a measure of its appeal after World War II, this genre was revived by Luciano Berio in a highly original manner in his *Folk Songs.* The eleven pieces in this collection take their tunes and words from traditional songs of America, Armenia, France, Italy, and Azerbaijan. The *Folk Songs* were written by Berio for the soprano Cathy Berberian, with whom he collaborated on numerous compositions of the 1950s and 1960s.

As folk songs go, the tune of "Black Is the Color of My True Love's Hair" is of recent origin. It was composed between 1916 and 1921 by the American folk singer John Jacob Niles (1892–1980). "I had come home from eastern Kentucky singing this song to an entirely different tune," he writes. "So I wrote a new tune, ending it in a nice modal manner." In Berio's treatment, the voice is accompanied by harp, cello, and viola, the last of which plays in the twangy manner of a "country dance fiddler." The viola part is not rhythmically synchronized with the vocal line.

Berio rearranged his *Folk Songs* for soprano and orchestra in 1973.

Bibliography

Music of the Twentieth Century, Chapter 15.

Discography

Cathy Berberian, soprano; Juilliard Ensemble, Luciano Berio, conductor. RCA Red Seal LSC 3189 (1971).
(Also see the recording by John Jacob Niles, voice and dulcimer, of this song: Traditional Carols and Love Songs, Traditional Records, TLP 1023, ca. 1957.)

*) Play section between repeat signs to signal ⊕. Section need not to be completed

© Copyright 1968 by Universal Edition (London) Ltd., London. All rights reserved. Used by permission of European American Music Distributors Corporation, sole U.S. agent for Universal Edition.

*) see preceding note

segue sino al segno
Viola
Voce
he no more on earth will be 't will sure - ly be the
Arpa
senza sord.
♩ = 72
4
mf
rall.
5
con sord.
end of me
black black black
*) ♩=92 (dalla 2a volta rallentare poco a poco sino a ♩ = 54)
(c.s.)
sempre pp e alla punta
is the col - our of my true love's hair his lips are something
*) see preceding note

gue fino al segno
Viola
Voce
ro - sy fair the sweet - est smile and the kind - - est
Arpa
senza sord.
mf
hands I love the grass where - on the stands
6
♩ = 92
rall.
mf
Vcello
pp
poco rall.
mf
p
pp

◆ 17 ◆

Peter Maxwell Davies (1934–)

Eight Songs for a Mad King *(1969):*
"Country Dance (Scotch Bonnett)"

The insanity of the English monarch George III is the subject of *Eight Songs for a Mad King,* a piece of musical theater composed by Peter Maxwell Davies to words by Randolph Stow. The part of the king is recited, sung, and acted. A flutist, clarinetist, violinist, and cellist play their parts from inside cages, by which they represent bullfinches that the king coached in singing. The ensemble also includes keyboard instruments and percussion, the latter of which represents the king's keeper.

In the seventh song, "Country Dance," the people of Windsor are regaled by the king's mad rendition of "Comfort Ye My People" from Handel's *Messiah.* The monarch's good spirits then lead to a foxtrot. But his mood becomes hysterical as his thoughts turn to the sinfulness and evil of the world. He takes the violin, which he plays and finally breaks apart, representing the destruction of his own soul.

Bibliography

Music of the Twentieth Century, Chapter 15.

Griffiths, Paul. *Peter Maxwell Davies,* pp. 64–66 and 147–49 (the latter consisting of notes by the composer). London, 1982.

Harvey, Jonathan. "Maxwell Davies's *Songs for a Mad King.*" *Tempo,* 89 (1969), 2–6.

Discography

Julius Eastman, voice; The Fires of London, Peter Maxwell Davies, conductor. Nonesuch H 71285 (1973).

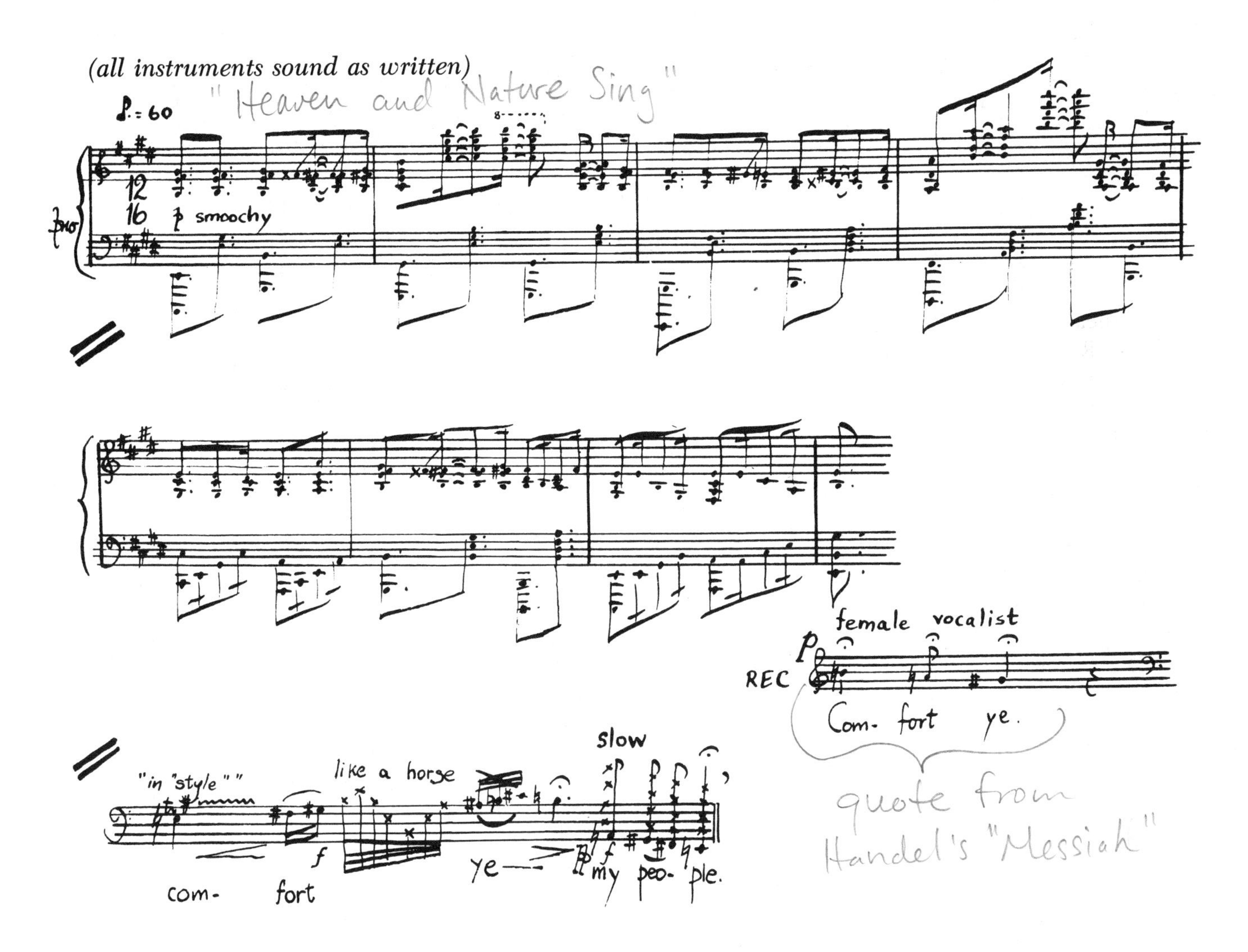

© Copyright 1971 by Boosey & Hawkes, Inc. Reprinted by permission.

fl.
cl
pc
tamb.
pno
improvise arpeggios over whole keyboard.
vln
arco
vlc
JAZZ CHORDS
Possibly from Wizard of OZ "Somewhere over the Rainbow"
"FOXTROT SECTION"
improvise band kit
use cupped hands as megaphone & bawl.
Recit
With sin-ging & with dan-cing, with milk & with ap-ples.
pz.

perc
(on)
pno
T.
The land-lord of the 3 Tuns makes best purl in the
hot beer w/
vln
ff vib. esagg.
vlc.
fl
mf
cl
mf
large cymbs
b. d's & tam tam only, simile
perc
(on.)
pno
T
Windsor
grabs after vln
vln
vlc

Bartók-like
pizz. w/ snap

fl
cresc
cl
cresc
cresc
let ring.
pno
cresc
v.
Sin!
sin!
sin!
takes vln from violinist
vlc
cresc
fff
♪ = 52
pno.
con Ped
v.
regal
black vice, in-to-le-ra-ble vile-ness in lanes, by ricks, at
becoming hysterical
plays vln with fingers in exaggerated pizzicato

small b.d. (pedal)
v. large bass dr
tamtam
complete darkness (many tone clusters)
Ped
Courts.
on wires, plectrum
intermittently stroke wood metal and glass jingles, & lower register of xyl, muffled.
repeat intermittently, becoming quieter.
hold
Ped off!
vln breaks apart
recit
It is night on the world. E-ven I, yr. King, have
basic ♩= 52
stop
harpsich.
off.
con- tem- pla- ted e- vil.
silky.
I shall rule with a rod of iron.
The King is referring to himself as "The Messiah"
vlc
Com- fort ye.

CODA
♪.= 48
FL
CL
sord
VLC
mp
PERC
jingles
recit
HPS
12-tone

PART III DRAMATIC AND ORCHESTRAL MUSIC

• 18 •

Richard Strauss (1864–1949)

Salome *(1903–1905): Final Scene*

Richard Strauss conceived his daring plan to use Oscar Wilde's play *Salomé* as an opera text even before he saw the play performed in 1903 at Max Reinhardt's Deutsches Theater. His impression at that performance only strengthened his resolve to bring to the operatic stage a story that mingled Biblical legend and perverse sexuality.

Wilde uses the Gospel accounts of the imprisonment and execution of John the Baptist at the hands of King Herod as a pretext for a grotesque fantasy of forbidden love. Herod's stepdaughter Salome develops an unquenchable lust for the ascetic Jochanaan (John the Baptist), and, following a seductive "Dance of the Seven Veils" for the pleasure of the king, she is granted her wish to be given the decapitated head of this prophet.

In her final soliloquy, Salome sings to the head, which she fondles and—in the darkness of a cloudy night—finally kisses. A beam of moonlight betrays her, and Herod, at last revulsed, commands that she be killed.

Bibliography

Music of the Twentieth Century, Chapter 7.

Del Mar, Norman. *Richard Strauss: A Critical Commentary on his Life and Works*, vol. 1, pp. 238–86. London, 1962.

Mann, William. *Richard Strauss: A Critical Study of the Operas*, pp. 39–62. New York, 1966.

Discography

Montserrat Caballé, Regina Resnik, Sherrill Milnes; London Symphony Orchestra, Erich Leinsdorf, conductor. RCA Red Seal LSC 7053 (1969).

Birgit Nilsson, Eberhard Wächter; Vienna Philharmonic Orchestra, Georg Solti, conductor. London OS 1218 (1970).

Gwyneth Jones, Dietrich Fischer-Dieskau; Hamburg Staatsoper, Karl Böhm, conductor. Deutsche Grammophon 2707052 (1971).

Hildegard Behrens, José Van Dam; Vienna Philharmonic Orchestra, Herbert von Karajan, conductor. Angel SBLX 3848 (1978).

Berlin: Adolph Fürstner, 1905. Piano reduction by Otto Singer.

5
Sal.
Ah! Du woll-test mich nicht deinen Mund küs-sen lassen,
Ah! thou wouldst not suf-fer me to kiss thy mouth, thou wouldst not,
p
Jocha-na-an!
Jo-ka-na-an!
10
Wohl,
Well,
cresc.
ff
più lento
Etwas breit.
ritard.
ich werde ihn jetzt küs-sen.
well, it shall now be kiss-ed.
M. ♩= 60
dim.
f
15
ff

Sal.
20
Ich will mit meinen Zäh - nen hin-
And with my teeth I'll bite it I
acceler.
espr.
ein - beis - - - sen,
will bite it
wie man in ei-ne rei - - fe Frucht beis-
as one bites in a ripe fruit. I
dim.
p
espr.
cresc.
25
- sen mag.
said I would.
sfz
ritard.
più largo
noch breiter
molto espr.
p
pp
Ja, ich will ihn jetzt
Yes I will kiss
f molto dim.

poco a poco più a tempo primo
wieder allmählich im Zeitmass.
30
Sal.
küs-sen, dei - - - - nen Mund, Jo-cha-na-an.
it now, kiss thy mouth, Jo-ka-na-an.
espr.
pp
Ich hab' es ge-sagt.
I said that I would.
espr.
p
35
Hab' ich's nicht gesagt?
Did I not say it?
Ja, ich hab' es ge-
Yes, yes, so I have
cresc.
sagt.
said.
Ah! Ah!
Ich will ihn jetzt
I will now kiss
f
ppp

40
Sal.
— küs - - - - - - sen...
— kiss thy mouth.
etwas fliessender
un poco più mosso
M. ♩ = 72
espr.
pp
ppp
45
A-ber wa-rum siehst du mich nicht an, Jo-cha-
But where-fore dost thou not look at me Jo-ka-
- na-an? Deine Au- - - gen, die so schreck- - - lich wa-ren
- na-an? Thine eyes that were so ter- - - - ri - ble,
50
smorzando
so voller Wut und Verachtung, sind jetzt geschlossen. Warum sind sie ge-
so full of rage and contempt, they are now closed Wherefore then are they
p
sfz
pp
espr.
mf
smorz.

ritard.
a tempo
Sal.
schlossen? Öff-ne doch die Au-gen, so he-be dei-ne Li-der, Jo-cha-
clo-sèd? O-pen thou thine eyes, lift up a-gain thine eye-lids, Jo-ka-
pp
p marc.
pp
55
- - na-an! Wa-rum siehst du mich nicht an? Hast du
- - na-an! Why dost thou not look at me? Art thou a-
molto espr.
tr
dim.
f
60
Angst vor mir, Jo-cha-na-an, dass du mich nicht an-
fraid of me? Jo-ka-na-an that thou wilt not look
p espr.
cresc
f
calando
a tempo M. 𝅗𝅥 = 72
-se-hen willst? Und dei-ne Zun-ge, sie
at me? And thy red tongue doth
(kurz und hart)
dim
p
espr cantabile
p
pp

65
Sal.
sprichtkein Wort,_ Jo-cha - - na-an, die-se Scharlachnat-ter, die ih-ren
speak no word, Jo-ka - - na-an, that scar-let vi-per spattingits
(sotto)
Sal.
Gei - fer ge-gen mich spie. Es ist selt-sam, nicht?
poi - son, it stirs no more. It is stran-ge, aye?
cresc.
pp
Sal.
Wie kommt es, dass die-se ro-te Nat-ter sich
How is it that this small scarlet vi-per doth
cresc.
70
Sal.
nicht mehr rührt?_
stir no more?_
dim.
p
espr.

Sal.
Du sprachst bö-se Wor-te ge-gen mich, ge-gen
Thou didst use e-vil lan-guage a-gainst me, a-gainst
cresc.
75
mich, Sa-lo-me, die Toch-ter der He-ro-di-as, Prin-zes-sin von Ju-
me, Sa-lo-mé, the daughter of He-ro-di-as, Prin-cess of Ju-
fp cresc.
marc
accelerando
più mosso
80 Ziemlich lebhaft.
dä-a.
dae-a.
Nun wohl!
Well then!
M. 𝅗𝅥 = 96
f
Ich le-be noch, a-ber du bist tot, und dein Kopf,
I'm li-ving still, but thou art dead, and thy head,
ff
sfz

85
immer bewegter.
sempre più mosso
Sal.
dein Kopf ge-hört mir! Ich kann mit ihm tun,
thy head belongs to me! I'm free to do with
ff
p
sfz
f
it
was ich will. Ich kann ihn den Hun - den vor - wer - fen
what I will. I may give it the dogs to feed on,
sfz
mf
90
und den Vö - geln der Luft. Was die Hun - - - - - de
and the birds in the air. What is left by
f
dim.
sfz
üb - rig las-sen, sol-len die Vö - gel der Luft
the dogs may be de - voured by the birds
p

Sal.
ver - zeh - ren....
of the air.
95
cresc.
accelerando molto
Ah! Ah! Jo - cha - na -
Ah! Ah! Jo - ka - na -
molto cresc.
ff
100
poco ritardando
an, Jo - cha - na - an, du warst
an, Jo - ka - na - an, thou wert
dim
espr.
Un poco mosso
Zart bewegt.
schön.
fair!
M. 𝅗𝅥 = 52
105
Dein Leib war ei - ne El -
Thy bo - dy was a co -
p (sehr singend)
pp
Ped. tenuto

Sal.
fen-bein-säu - le auf sil-ber-nen Füs - - - sen. Er war ein
lumn of i - vo-ry set on a sil - - - ver socket. It was a
pp
110
Gar - ten vol-ler Tau - ben in der Sil - ber-li - - lien
gar - den full of do - ves, full of sil - ver li - - lies'
cresc.
dim.
sempre piu mosso
immer fliessender im Zeitmass.
molto appassionato
115
Glanz. Nichts in der Welt war so weiss wie dein
shine. No thing on earth was so white as thy
pp
cresc.
fespr.
dim.
Leib. Nichts in der Welt war so schwarz wie dein
skin. No thing on earth was so black as thy
p
f
fp
dim.

120
Sal.
Haar. In der gan - zen Welt war nichts
hair. And in all the world was no -
espr
pp
cresc.
f
ritard.
125
Un poco più tranquillo
(ma sempre alla breve)
Etwas ruhiger (aber stets ¢).
so rot wie dein Mund.
-thing so red as thy mouth.
M. 𝅗𝅥 = 44
pp
dim.
p
marc
130
Dei - ne Stim - me war ein Wei -
But thy voice was a cen -
pp
marc.
p
pp
accelerando
135
- rauch - ge - fäss und wenn ich dich
- ser of sweet scents, and when I looked
marc.
pp
marc.

ritard.
più ritard.
lento (sempre ¢)
langsam (stets ¢).
140
Sal.
an-sah, hör - te ich ge-heim - nis-vol-le Mu - sik...
on thee I could hear a mu - sic of strange sounds
dim.
pp
espr.
145
cresc.
dim.
(Lost in thought as she gazes upon Jokanaan's head)
(In den Anblick von Jochanaans Haupt versunken.)
150
Ah!
Ah!
Wa-rum
Wherefore
l.H.
pp
mfespr.
ritard.
a tempo
155
hast du mich nicht an - ge - sehn, Jo - cha -
didst thou ne - ver look at me, Jo - ka -
pp
allmählich fliessender.
poco accelerando
un poco più mosso
Etwas bewegter. M. ♩= 60.
- na - an? Du leg - test ü - ber dei - ne Au - gen die
- na - an? Thou didst put u - pon thine eyes the
p
espr.

160
sempre più vivo
immer lebhafter.
Sal.
Bin - de ei - - - nes, der sei - nen Gott schau - en woll -
cov'ring of him who seek - eth God in all His glo -
p espr.
165
170
- te. Wohl! Du hast dei-nen Gott ge-sehn, Jo-cha - - na-an,
- - ry. Well! Thou may'st have seen thy God, Jo-ka - - na-an,
fp
pp
accelerando
a - ber mich, mich, mich
but me, me, me,
cresc.
f
175
molto espr.
sempre più mosso
immer bewegter.
hast du nie ge - sehn. Hät-test du
thou didst ne - ver see. If thou hadst
espr.
p

180
Sal.
mich ge-sehn, du hät - test mich ge - liebt!
looked at me, thou wouldst have loved
cresc.
appassionato
Sehr bewegt. M. 𝅗𝅥 = 80
me.
Molto mosso
Ich dür - ste nach dei - ner
I'm thir - sting for all thy
ff
p
185
Schön - heit. Ich hung - re nach dei - nem
beau - ty. I'm hun - gry for thy bo - -
f
pp
190
Leib. Nicht Wein noch Äp - fel kön - - nen mein Ver - lan - gen
dy. Neither wine nor app - les can ap - pease all my de -
cresc.
espr.
dim.

195
stringendo
Mit grosser Steigerung
Sal.
stil - len...
stire
Was soll ich jetzt tun, Jo-cha -
What shall I do now, Jo-ka -
espr.
p
cresc.
p
200
- na-an?
- na-an?
Nicht die Flu - ten, noch die gro - ssen
Not by floods nor by the great
cresc.
Was - ser kön - nen die-ses brün - - - - sti-ge Be-
wa - ters can e - ver the heat of my strong
205
cresc.
f
molto allegro
sehr lebhaft
210
geh - ren lö - - - schen...
passion be quen - - - chèd
Oh!
Oh!
Wa-rum
Wherefore
ff

Sal.
sahst du mich nicht an?
didst thou not look at me?
piu accelerando
Hät-test du
If thou hadst
cresc.
ff
sfz
215
mich an-ge-sehn du
look-ed at me thou
lento
mehr als doppelt so
hät-test mich ge-liebt.
wouldst have lov-ed me.
M. 𝅗𝅥 : 62
mf
cresc.
ff
p
espr.
220
langsam.
Ich weiss es wohl, du hät-test mich ge-
I know it well, thou wouldst have lov-ed
cresc
molto
ff
225
liebt.
me,
molto ritenuto
Und das Ge-heim-nis der Lie-
and the great mys-te-ry of love
dim.
p
dim.
pp

230
Sal.
- - - be ist grö - sser als das Ge - heim - nis des
is grea - - ter than the myste - ry
dim.
ppp
pp
235
mässig bewegt
moderato
To - des...
of death...
M. 𝅗𝅥 = 80.
pp
ppp
Herod (with lowered voice to Herodias)
Herodes (leise zu Herodias.)
240
Sie ist ein Un-ge-heu-er, dei-ne Tochter. Ich sa-ge dir, sie ist ein
She is a hi-deous monster, thy daughter. I tell it thee, she's al-to-
Herodias (powerful) (stark.)
Meine Tochter hat recht ge-tan. Ich möch - te jetzt hier bleiben.
I approve of my daugh-ter's deed. And I will now stay here.
Hero-des.
Un-ge-heuer!
gether monstrous!
Ah!
Ah!
ff
dim.
ff sfz
trem.

Herodes.
Da spricht meines Bruders Weib.
There speaks my brother's wife.
(weaker)
(schwächer)
Komm, ich will nicht an diesem Orte bleiben.
Come, I will no longer stay in this place.
dim.
p
245
(vehemently)
(heftig)
Komm, sag ich dir!
Come, I tell thee!
Si-cher, es wird
Sure-ly, something
ff p
ff
Schreck-li-ches ge-schehn.
ter-ri-ble will happen.
Wir wol-len uns im Pa-last ver-ber-gen,
Let us hide ourselves in the pa-lace,
He-ro-di-as, ich fan-ge
He-ro-di-as, I am be-
mf
250
(der Mond verschwindet)
an zu er-zit-tern...
ginning to tremble...
(the moon disappears)
p
sf
f
mf

doppelt so schnell. molto allegro (doppio movimente)
(auffahrend) (rising suddenly)
Herodes.
Man - nas - sah, Is - sa - char, O - zi - as, löscht die
Ma - nas - seh, I - sa - char, O - zi - as, put out the
Fa - ckeln aus. Ver - bergt den Mond, ver - bergt die Ster - ne!
tor - ches. Hide the moon, hide the stars
255
(the stage becomes very dark)
(es wird ganz dunkel)
Es wird Schreck - li - ches ge - schehn.
Something ter - ri - ble will come.
260
marc.
cresc.
ff
Lento
doppelt so langsam.
dim.
pp
poco f
265
270
Salome (matt.) sehr gedehnt M. ♩= 58.
(faintly)
Ah! Ich ha - be dei - nen Mund ge - küsst. Jo - cha -
Ah! I have kissed thy mouth, Jo - ka -

Sal.
- na-an.
- na-an.
Ah!
Ah!
Ich ha-be ihn ge-küsst, dei-nen
I have kissed thy
pp
p
275
Mund, es war ein bit-te-rer Ge-schmack auf dei-nen Lip-pen
mouth, there was a bit-ter, bit-ter taste on thy red lips.
280
Hat es nach Blut ge-schmeckt?
Was it the taste of blood?
Nein! Doch es schmeck-te viel-leicht nach
Nay! But per-chance this is the taste of
mf
espr.
pp
285
Lie-be...
love...
molto espr.
mf

290
Sal.
Sie sa-gen, dass die Lie- -be bit - ter schmecke...
They say that love hath a bit - ter taste...
mf
Al-lein was tut's?
But what of that?
Was tut's?
What of that?
molto espr.
mf
f
p
295
Ich ha-be deinen Mund ge-
I have now kissed thy
M. 𝅗𝅥 = 60.
ff
küsst, Jo-cha - na - an. Ich ha-be ihn ge-küsst
mouth, Jo-ka - na - an. I have now kissed
300
dim.
molto espr.

ritard.
molto largo
sehr breit
305
(A moonbeam falls
(Der Mond bricht
Sal.
dei - - nen Mund.
thy mouth.
ff
sfz
on Salome, covering her with light.)
wieder hervor und beleuchtet Salome.)
Herod (turning round)
Herodes (sich umwendend)
schneller
frei
Man tö - - te die-ses
Go, kill at once that
ritard.
più mosso
dim.
sfz
Molto allegro
Sehr schnell.
(Die Soldaten stürzen sich auf Salome
und begraben sie unter ihren Schilden.)
Herodes.
Weib!
wench!
(The soldiers rush forward and
crush Salomé under their shields.)
M. 𝅗𝅥 = 80.
315
(Courtain.)
(Der Vorhang fällt schnell.)
320

◆ 19 ◆

Igor Stravinsky (1882–1971)

Petrushka *(1910–11): Second Scene*

Petrushka is Stravinsky's second ballet score written for Sergei Diaghilev and the Ballets Russes and the first that clearly reveals his musical personality. The scenario of the ballet, devised by the composer in collaboration with Alexandre Benois, is in four connected scenes. At a nineteenth-century Shrovetide fair in St. Petersburg, a showman reveals his puppets—the clown Petrushka, a ballerina, and a Moor—who come to life at the sound of the showman's flute. In the second scene Petrushka curses his lot in life; the ballerina brings tender thoughts to his mind, but she deserts him and he again cries out in rage. The ballerina now visits the exotic Moor, whom she seduces. Petrushka bursts in upon their amorous scene, but he is promptly thrown out by the Moor. After witnessing a succession of dance numbers in the final scene, the crowd at the fair is shocked to see Petrushka pursued and murdered by the Moor. The showman reasserts that Petrushka is only a puppet, but as he drags the lifeless body back to his tent, Petrushka's ghost is seen thumbing his nose at the crowd.

The music of the second scene was conceived in 1910 as a concert piece for piano and orchestra and subsequently revised as part of the ballet. The music was further revised by Stravinsky in 1947, although the score presented here is from the original version of the ballet.

Bibliography

Music of the Twentieth Century, Chapter 8.

Benois, Alexandre. *Reminiscences of the Russian Ballet*, pp. 324–26 and passim. Trans. Mary Britnieva. London, 1941.

Fokine, Michel. *Memoirs of a Ballet Master*, pp. 183–94. Trans. Vitale Fokine, ed. Anatole Chujoy. Boston and Toronto, 1961.

Hamm, Charles, ed. *Stravinsky: Petrushka.* Norton Critical Scores. New York, 1967. Contains articles and reviews and the complete score of the first edition with corrections.

Toorn, Pieter C. Van den. *The Music of Igor Stravinsky*, pp. 31–98. New Haven, London, 1983.

White, Eric Walter. *Stravinsky: The Composer and his Works*, pp. 193–203. Berkeley, Los Angeles, 1979.

Discography (1911 version only)

New Philharmonia Orchestra, Erich Leinsdorf, conductor. London STS 15478 (1971).

New York Philharmonic, Pierre Boulez, conductor. Columbia M 31076 (1971).

London Symphony Orchestra, Charles Dutoit, conductor. Deutsche Grammophon 2530771; cassette 3300711 (1977).

London Symphony Orchestra, Claudio Abbado, conductor. Deutsche Grammophon 2532010 (digital); 400042-2 GH (compact disc) (1981).

London Symphony Orchestra, Bernard Haitink, conductor. Philips 412371-1 (1984).

At the rise of the curtain, the door in Petrushka's room opens suddenly. A foot kicks him on to the stage. Petrushka falls and the door closes behind him.

*) *For concert performance, this drum part is omitted.*

Berlin: Russischer Musikverlag, 1912.

49
Molto meno. 𝅗𝅥= 50.
Cl. I.(Si♭)
Cl. II.(LA)
Fag. I. II.
I. SOLO.
mf lamentoso
Tr. I.
Solo lamentoso assai
sord.
V. I.
pizz.
49
Allegro. 𝅗𝅥= 76.
Piano.
Soli con sord.
senza sord.
50
Cl. I. = LA
Colla parte
50

Furious
Furioso.
51
Curses of Petrushka
Fl. I.
Fl. II.
trem.
Ob. I. II.
Cor. Ingl.
Cl. I. (la)
Cl. II. (la)
Cl. III. (la)
Fag. I.
Fag. II.
Fag. III.
bouchés (cuivrez)
Cor. I. II.
Cor. III. IV.
Pist. I. II. (sord.)
Tr. I. II. (sord.)
a 2.
(secouez)
Tamb. de Basque.
DANS LA COULISSE. (COME SOPRA)
Tamb. milit. et Tambourin
Piano.
Furioso.
V. I.
détachés
V. II.
Viole.
Celli.
51

Fl. I.
Fl. II.
Ob. I. II.
Cor. Ingl.
Cl. I.
Cl. II.
Cl. III.
Fag. I.
Fag. II.
Fag. III.
Cor. I. II.
Cor. III. IV.
Pist. I. II.
Tr. I. II.
3 Trb.
Sordini a 3.
fff
Tamb. de Basque.
Tamb. milit. et Tambourin.
Piano.
ff
V. I.
V. II.
Viole.
Celli.

#52-54
Stable Sect.
52
Adagietto. ♪= 54.
Solo dolente
Fl. picc. I.
Fl. I.
Fl. II.
Ob. I. II.
Cor. Ingl.
Cl. I.
Cl. II.
Cl. III.
Fag. I.
Fag. II.
Fag. III.
Cor. I. II.
Cor. III. IV.
Pist. I. II.
Tr. I. II.
3 Trb. e Tuba.
Timp.
Xyliph.
Tamb. de Basque.
Piano.
V. I.
V. II.
Viole.
Celli.
C. B.
molto
secco
quasi gliss.
non cresc.
div.
pizz.
D

D lydian
53 Andantino.
Accel.
Fl. I-II.
Cor. Ingl.
Cl. I.
Cl. II. III.
Tr. I.
I. (Sord)
Cl. I = Si♭
Cl. II. III = Si♭
dolente
cresc.
Andantino.
poco ten.
f sub.
p sub.
Piano.
A
B
C#
D
E
F#
G#
A
53
Fl. I.
54
Solo.
Cl. basso.
Fag. II.
Piatti e Gr. Cassa.
stacc.
sim.
con sord.
sord.
V. I.
V. II.
(pizz.)
.C.B.
54

55
Solo.
dolce mf
Fl. I.
Cor. Ingl.
Cl. basso.
SOLO.
I.
II.
mf dolente
Fag. I. II.
Piatti.
Gr. Cassa.
m.s.
p sempre
Piano.
senza sord.
V. I.
senza sord.
V. II.
con sord.
Viole.
con sord.
C.B.
55
The ballerina enters
Meno mosso. 𝅗𝅥 = 72.
Fl. picc. I.
p
Fl. I.
p
Fag. I. II.
Meno mosso. 𝅗𝅥 = 72.
rit.
senza sord.
senza sord.
Viole.

56
Allegro. ♩ = 100.
Fl. Picc. I.
Fl. I. II.
Ob. I. II.
a 2.
Cor. Ingl.
Cl. I. II.
f staccato
marc.
f stacc.
Cl. III.
Fag. I.
Fag. II. III.
ma non troppo
Cor. II. IV.
simile
Pist. I.
senza sord.
Solo
mf marcato
(con sord.)
Tr. I. II.
Timp.
Arpe I. II. a 2
Piano.
V. I.
div.
unis
poco sf
V. II.
pizz.
arco
Viole.
Celli.
C. B.
56

57
Fl. Picc. I.
Fl. I. II.
Ob. I. II.
Cor. Ingl.
Cl. I. II.
Cl. III.
Fag. I.
Fag. II. III.
Cor. I. II.
Cor. III. IV.
Pist. I. II.
Tr. I. II.
Timp.
Arpa I.
Arpa II.
Piano.
V. I.
V. II.
Viole.
Celli.
C.B.
stacc.
a 2.
arco
pizz.
(pizz.)
sim.
57

58 The ballerina leaves
crescendo
Fl. Picc. I. II.
Fl. I. II.
Ob. I. II. III.
Cor. Ingl.
Cl. I. II.
Cl. III.
Fag. I.
Fag. II. III.
Cor. I. II.
Cor. III. IV.
Pist. I. II.
Tr. I. II.
3 Trb.
Arpa I.
Arpa II.
Piano.
V. I.
V. II.
Viole.
Celli.
C. B.
stacc.
ten.
sempre sim.
cuivrez
con sord.
simile
sempre
sim.
arco
div.
unis
detaché
pizz.
58

Ad libitum.
Fl. Picc. I. II.
Fl. I. II.
Ob. I. II. III.
Cor. Ingl.
Colla parte del Pianoforte.
Cl. I. II.
simile
ten.
fff Cadenza
molto ritard.
p lamentoso assai
Cl. III.
Fag. I.
Fag. II. III.
Cor. I. II.
Cor. III. IV.
Pist. I. II.
Tr. I. II.
Trb. I. II. III.
Timp.
Arpa I.
Arpa II.
Piano.
Colla parte del Clarinetto.
string.
V. I.
V. II.
Viole.
Celli.
arco
pizz.
C. B.

59
Vivo stringendo. ♩= 100.
Lento. Tempo.
Lento. Tempo.
Cor. Ingl.
p (tranquillo)
sim.
Piano.
mf
crescendo
Cl. I.
Cl. II.
Arpa I.
Piano.
V. I.
Fl. Picc. I.
Fl. I.
Fl. II.
Arpa II.
ff

60
Petrushka's despair
Fl. I.
Fl. II.
Ob. I. II.
Cor. Ingl.
Cl. I.
Cl. II.
Cl. III.
Fag. I.
Fag. II.
Fag. III.
I. II. bouchés (cuivrez)
Cor. I. II.
III. bouchés (cuivrez)
Cor. III.
a 2.
Pist. I. II. (sord.)
Tr. I. II. (sord.)
Tamb. de Basque.
(secouez)
DANS LA COULISSE (come sopra).
Tamb. milit. et Tambourin.
Arpa I. II.
Piano.
V. I.
détachés
V. II.
détachés
Viole.
60

Fl. I.
Fl. II.
Ob. I. II.
Cor. Ingl.
Cl. I.
Cl. II.
Cl. III.
Fag. I.
Fag. II.
Fag. III.
Cor. I. II.
Cor. III.
Pist. I. II.
Tr. I. II.
Trb. I. II. III.
con sord. a 3.
fff
mf
p
Tamb. de Basque.
Tamb. milit. et Tambourin.
crescendo
Piano.
V. I.
V. II.
Viole.

61
Lento.
Più mosso. ♩= 84.
Curtain
Fl. I.
Fl. II.
Ob. I II.
Cor. Ingl.
Solo.
Cadenza (Lento)
Cl. I.
Cl. II.
Cl. III.
enharm.
dim.
Petrushka's Motive
Fag. I.
Fag. II.
Fag. III.
bouchés
Très lointain
Cor. I. II.
Cor. III. IV.
reference to the accordian
I. II. senza sord.
Solo
Pist. I. II.
Tr. I. II.
Timp.
Tambourin.
DANS LA COULISSE.
Très lointain.
(L'istesso tempo)
simile ad lib.
Piano.
V. I.
V. II.
Viole.
Celli.
C.B.
pizz.
più sf
F#

• 20 •

Alban Berg (1885–1935)

Lulu *(1928–35):*
"Lied der Lulu" (from Act 2, scene 1)

As a text for his opera *Lulu*, Berg adapted Frank Wedekind's Expressionistic dramas *Earth Spirit* and *Pandora's Box*. The central character of the first of these plays is Lulu, who represents the female life principle. She is married to a succession of men who fall totally under her spell, each of whom is destroyed by her seductivity. In the "Song of Lulu" she states her philosophy. Her apparent destructiveness, she tells her husband Dr. Schön, is a condition to which her victims willingly submit.

The Song is one of over fifty numbers into which the composer divides the three-act opera. The music exemplifies Berg's free adaptation of the twelve-tone method of composition and his use of several tone rows in addition to nonserial structures of pitches. Its vocal style is highly coloratura, which helps to express Lulu's seductivity.

Lulu was left incomplete at the time of Berg's death in 1935, lacking a completed orchestration of the third act and other minor revisions which he had planned. It has been performed in its entirety only since 1979, in a version completed by Friedrich Cerha. The music of the "Song of Lulu" also appears as the third movement in Berg's *Lulu* Suite (1934).

TEXT

If men have killed themselves on my account, my value is not lessened.
You knew why you married me, just as I knew why I married you.
You had cheated your best friends with me, so you could not cheat yourself with me.
If you sacrifice your latter years to me, so you have had my entire youth in return.
I have never wished to appear anything in the world other than that for which I am taken, and I have never been taken for anything else in the world than what I am.

Bibliography

Music of the Twentieth Century, Chapter 7.
Carner, Mosco. *Alban Berg: The Man and the Work*, pp. 215–76. 2d, rev. ed. New York, 1983.
Jarman, Douglas. *The Music of Alban Berg*, passim. Berkeley, 1979.
Perle, George. *The Operas of Alban Berg*. Vol. 2: *Lulu*. Berkeley, 1985.
Redlich, Hans. *Alban Berg*, pp. 163–202. London, 1957.
Reich, Willi. *Alban Berg*, pp. 156–77. Trans. Cornelius Cardew. New York, 1965.

Discography

Teresa Stratas, Yvonne Minton, Hanna Schwarz; Orchestre de l'Opéra de Paris, Pierre Boulez, conductor. Deutsche Grammophon 2711024 (complete opera, 1979).
Evelyn Lear, Dietrich Fischer-Dieskau; Orchester der Deutschen Oper, Karl Böhm, conductor. Deutsche Grammophon 139273/75 (lacks Act 3, 1968).

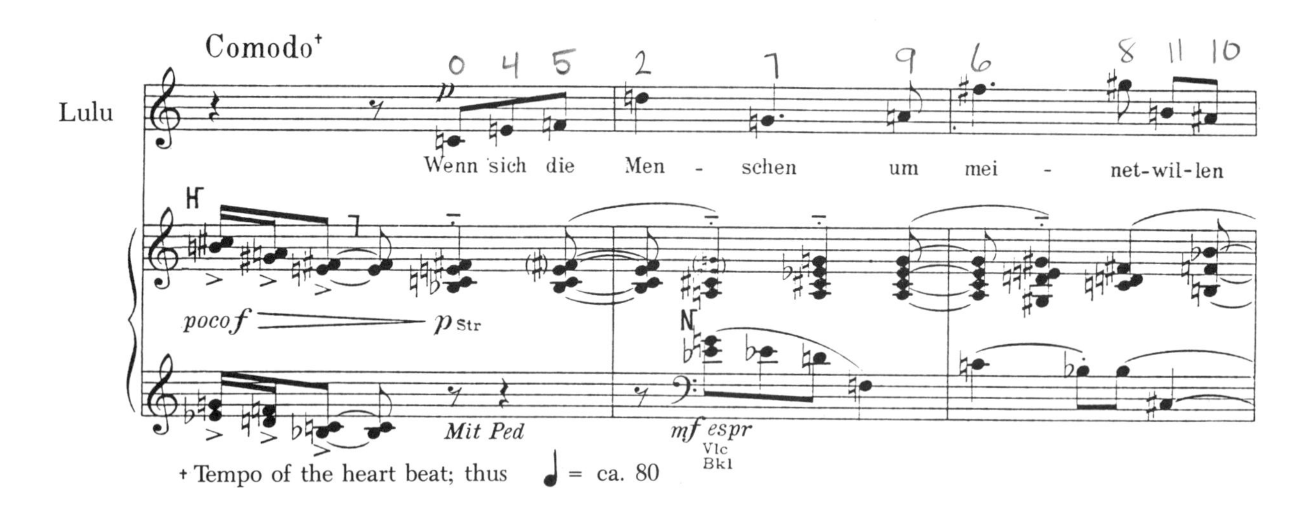

+ Tempo of the heart beat; thus ♩ = ca. 80

The Song of Lulu is dedicated to Anton von Webern on his fiftieth birthday.

Copyright 1936 by Universal Edition. © renewed 1964 by Universal Edition. All rights reserved. Used by permission of European American Music Distributors Corporation, sole U. S. agent for Universal Edition.

po
mf
Rubato
(poco rit.
L
Du hast so gut ge - wußt, wes-we - gen Du mich zur
500
Hr
mf
Str
3
poco
accel.)
a tempo
Frau nahmst, wie ich ge - wußt ha - be,
Sax
Hr
espr
mf
Vl
3
Rubato
(poco rit.
a tempo
poco accel.)
wes-we - gen ich Dich zum Mann nahm.
505
Str
Klav

OSSIA
be - - sten Freun -
Fl
Ossia
mf
Du
Du hat - test Dei - ne be - - sten Freun -
(poco allarg)
Trp
Ob Kl
p
Hfe

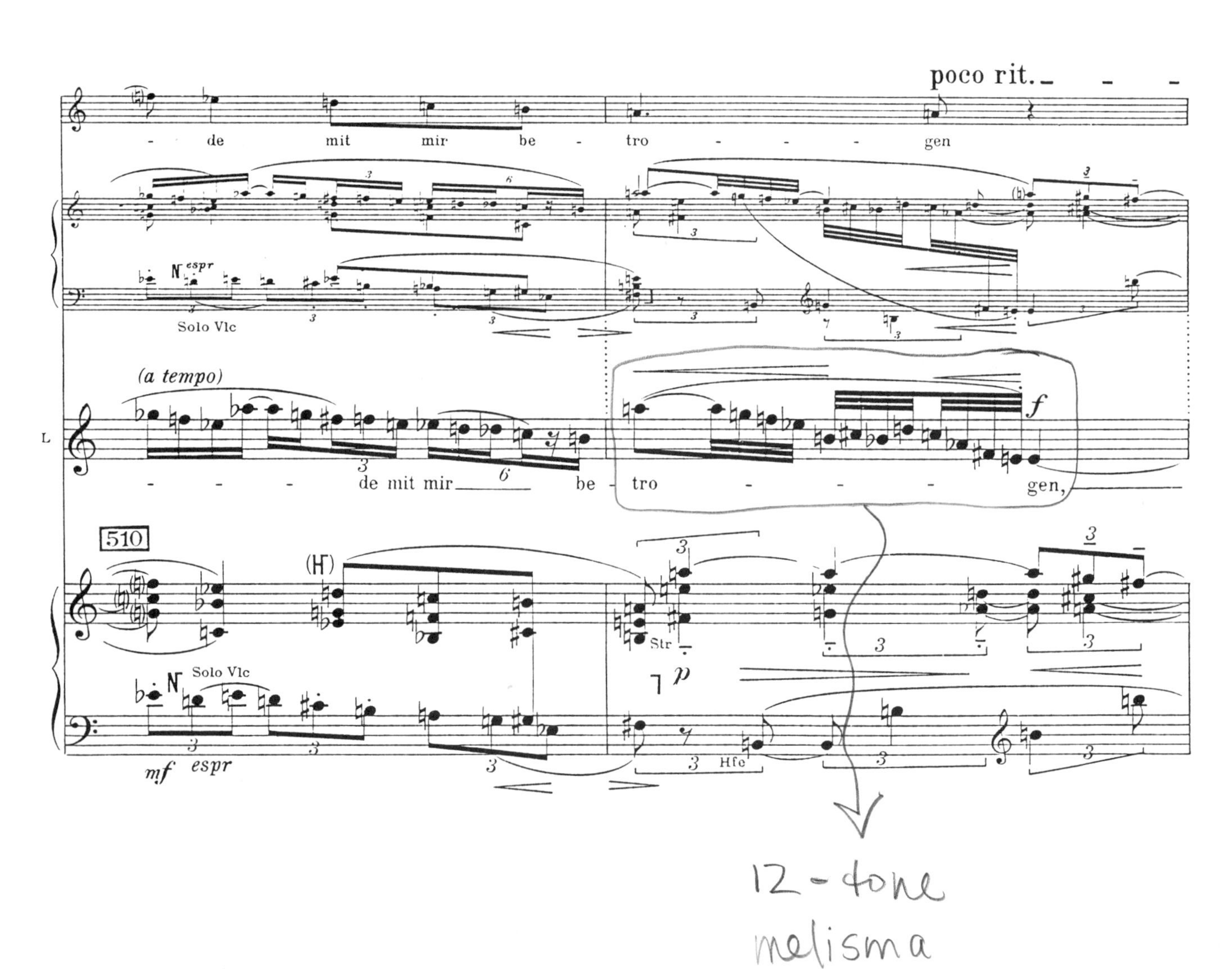
poco rit.
- de mit mir be - tro - - - - gen
espr
Solo Vlc
(a tempo)
- - - de mit mir be - tro - - - - gen,
f
510
Solo Vlc
Str
p
mf espr
Hfe
12-tone melisma

OSSIA
Dich
sel
Hfe
Fl
a tempo
Ossia
Du
L
Du konn - test nicht gut auch noch
Dich
sel
Trp
Hfe
Ob Kl
p
515
poco rit.
ber mit mir be - trü - - - - gen.
L
ber mit mir be - trü - - - - - gen.
Solo Vl
espr
p
Str
p

a tempo
poco rit.
L
Wenn Du mir Deinen Le - bens-a-bend zum Op-fer bringst,
Hr gest
mf
Vl
mp
a tempo
poco rit.
L
so hast Du mei-ne gan - - ze Ju-gend da-für ge-habt.
520
mf
a tempo
L
Ich Ich ha-be nie in der Welt
Solo Vl
Holzbl
Hr
marc
dolce
marc
Hfe
dolce
marc
525
L
et-was an - - de-res schei - - - - nen
Holzbl
dolce
marc
dolce
marc
dolce

wol - len, als wo - für man mich ge -
Vl
Holzbl
marc dolce marc dolce marc
Zeit lassen
rit.
a tempo
Ossia
nom - men
nom - men hat; und man hat mich
Str
mf
Hr
Holzbl u Klav
nie in der Welt für et-was an - - -
530
Fl
mp
Str
Trp
Pos
allarg.
- - - de - res ge - nom - - - - men,
Fl
Sax
espr
cresc
Auftakt
Hr

Etwas breiter
L
als
was
ich
bin.
Sax
Holzbl
dim sempre
535
Hr
poco f espr
Tba
Noch breiter
attacca
Vl
Sax
p
Hfe
Hr
Kl
Vla
Vlc
Pos
Fg

• 21 •

Dimitri Shostakovich (1906–75)

Lady Macbeth of the Mtsensk *(1930–32): Orchestral Interlude between scenes 4 and 5*

Lady Macbeth of the Mtsensk was intended by Shostakovich to be the first in a series of dramatic works focusing upon the place of women in the Soviet state. The opera is based upon a realistic nineteenth-century story by Nikolai Leskov in which Katerina Izmailova murders both her father-in-law and husband. Shostakovich's version uses Katerina's actions to symbolize women in Soviet society overthrowing the debasing conditions of their existence in Tsarist Russia.

Shostakovich's music is highly eclectic as it ranges from the sentimental and folk-like to moments of Expressionistic atonality and dissonance. Despite Shostakovich's protestations to the contrary, *Lady Macbeth* is indebted to German Expressionist opera and, especially, to Berg's *Wozzeck*, which Shostakovich saw performed in Leningrad in 1927. Both are works of social criticism in which violence is a symptom of human and social disintegration. Like *Wozzeck*, *Lady Macbeth* is cast into a continuous shape in which scenes within an act are connected by orchestral interludes with which they share common motives. This through-composed structure is balanced in both *Wozzeck* and *Lady Macbeth* by division of scenes into discrete musical forms or genres.

The musical climax of the opera occurs at its midpoint: the interlude separating the fourth and fifth scenes. Although it is connected by common motives to the love duet of scene 5, this interlude is a closed musical form—a passacaglia upon a ground bass introduced in measures 9–17. In an article for *Modern Music* (1935), Shostakovich describes the passacaglia as the place "in which the composer states his attitude toward the tragedy." It is thus comparable to the final interlude of Act 3 of Berg's *Wozzeck*, also a symphonic reflection by the composer upon the dramatic substance of his opera.

Lady Macbeth was immensely successful in the Soviet Union after its premiere in 1934, but it was withdrawn two years later when its style and subject were criticized by the Soviet government. It was revised and retitled *Katerina Izmailova* (op. 114) in 1963, at which time it returned to the operatic repertory in the Soviet Union.

Bibliography

Music of the Twentieth Century, Chapter 8.

Lebedinsky, L. Preface to the full score of *Katerina Izmailova*, vol. 1. Moscow, 1965.

Norris, Geoffrey. "The Operas." In *Shostakovich: The Man and his Music*, pp. 105–24. Ed. Christopher Norris. London, 1982.

Shostakovich, Dimitri. "My Opera *Lady Macbeth*." *Modern Music*, 12 (1935), 23–30.

Discography

Galina Vishnevskaya, Nicolai Gedda; London Philharmonic Orchestra, Mstislav Rostropovich, conductor. Angel SCLX-3866 (1979, orig. version).

Eleonora Andreyeva, Eduard Bulavin; Nemirovich-Danchenko Musical Drama Theater, Moscow, Gennady Provatorov, conductor. Melodiya/Angel RCL 4100 (1967, rev. version).

Used by arrangement with G. Schirmer, Inc. U.S. agent for Musikverlag Hans Sikorski, Hamburg.

271
Cl. b.
Fag.
a2
C-fag.
V-le
f espr.
V-c.
f espr.
div.
C-b.
10
15
Variation 1
Cl. b.
C-fag.
V-ni I
f espr.
V-c.
6
3
C-b.
20
272
Cl. b.
C-fag.
f espr.
Archi
f espr.
NEW RHYTHM
f espr.
25
Variation 2

Cl. b
C-fag.
V-le
V-c.
C-b.
CHANGE OF TIMBRE
f espr.
30
273
Inter-locking of viola + cello
f espr.
35
40
Variation 3
274
Arpe
V-ni II
Material from Var. 1
f espr.
45
Variation 4

Cl. b.
C-fag.
Arpe
8
V-ni II
V-le
V-o.
C-b.
50
275
Cl. b.
a2
Fag.
f espr.
C-fag.
Arpe
8
f espr.
Archi
Variation 5

Picc.
Fl.
Ob.
C.ingl.
Cl. p.
Cl.
Cl. b.
Fag.
C fag.
Cor.
Arpe
Archi
a 2
f
f espr.
3
8
55

Picc.
Fl.
Ob.
C.ingl.
Cl. p.
Cl.
Cl. b.
Fag.
C-fag.
Cor.
Arpe
Archi
a2
cresc.
sf
(loco)
60

276
Picc.
Fl.
a2
Ob.
C.ingl.
Cl. p.
Cl.
Cl. b.
Fag.
C-fag.
Cor.
Arpe
Archi
ff
Variation 6

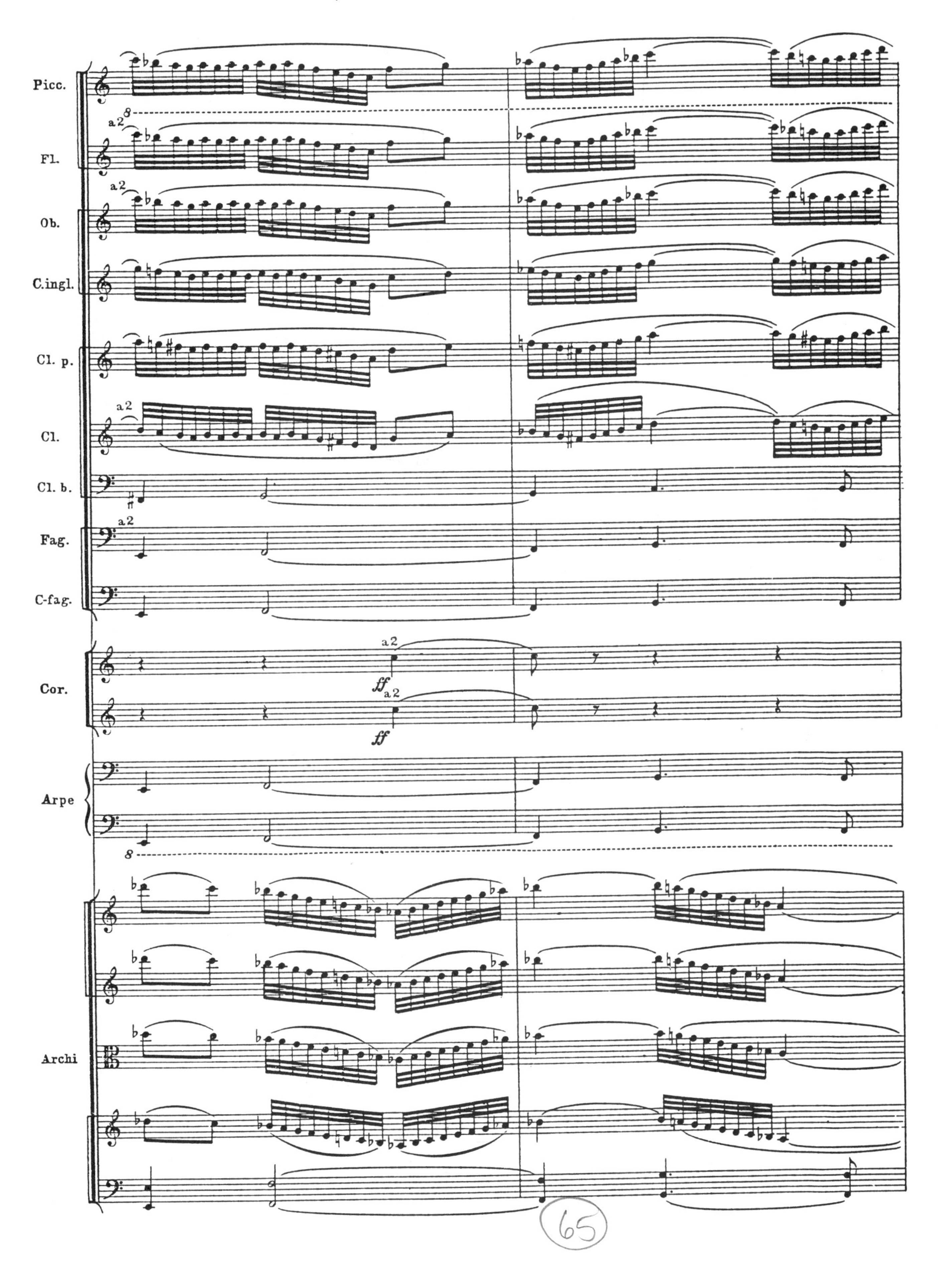
Picc.
Fl.
a2
Ob.
a2
C.ingl.
Cl. p.
Cl.
a2
Cl. b.
Fag.
a2
C-fag.
Cor.
a2
ff
a2
ff
Arpe
Archi

Picc.
Fl.
a2
Ob.
a2
C.ingl.
Cl. p.
Cl.
a2
Cl. b.
Fag.
a2
C-fag.
Cor.
II
f
IV
f
Tr-be
Tr-ni e Tuba
a2
f
p cresc.
Arpe
8
Archi

Picc.
Fl.
Ob.
C.ingl.
Cl. p.
Cl.
Cl. b.
Fag.
C.fag.
Cor.
Tr-be
Tr-ni
e
Tuba
Arpe
Archi
a2
II
IV
mf cresc.
f
cresc.

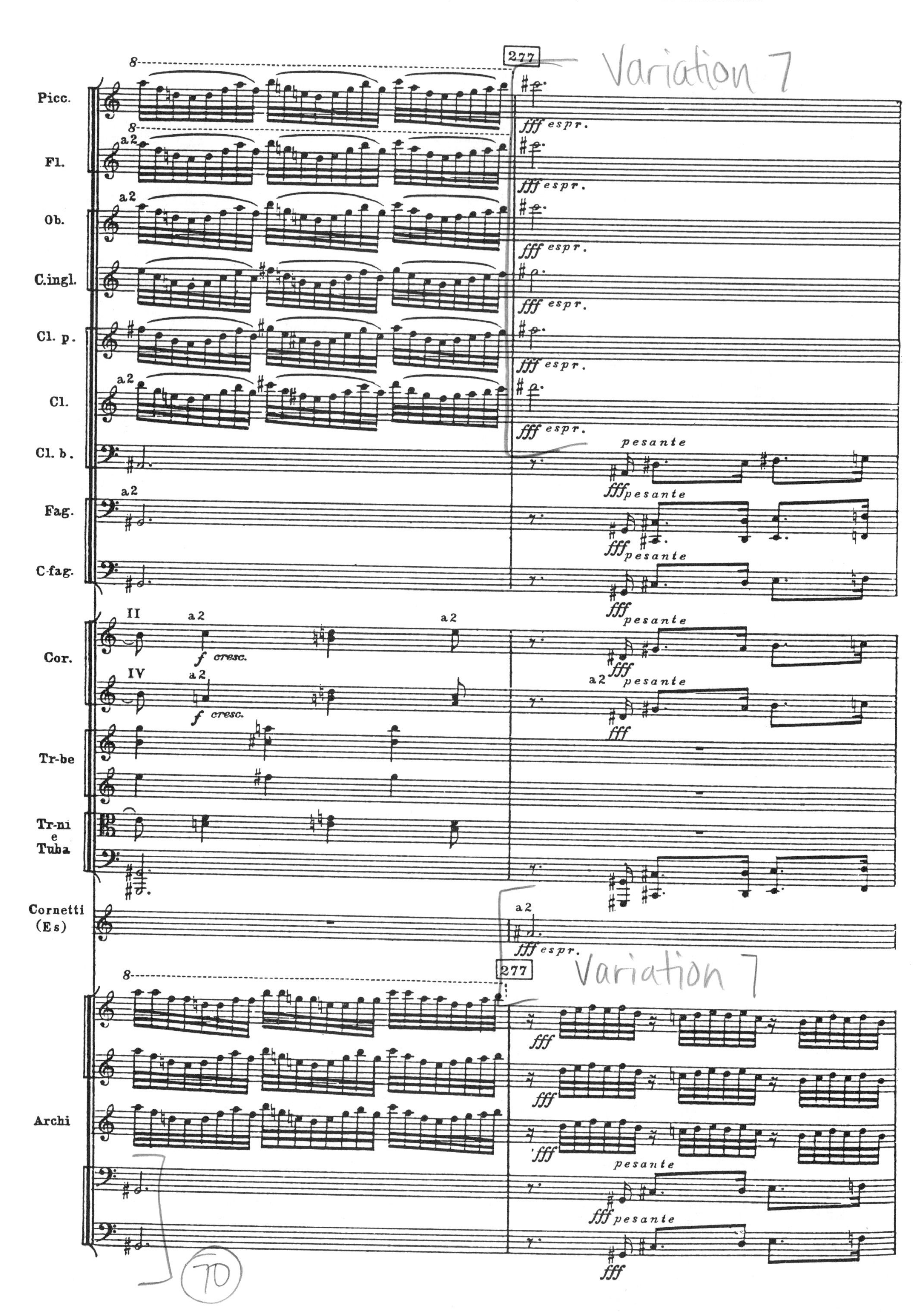
277
Variation 7
Picc.
Fl.
a2
Ob.
C.ingl.
Cl. p.
Cl.
Cl. b.
Fag.
C-fag.
fff espr.
pesante
fff
Cor.
II
IV
a2
f cresc.
Tr-be
Tr-ni e Tuba
Cornetti (Es)
Archi
70

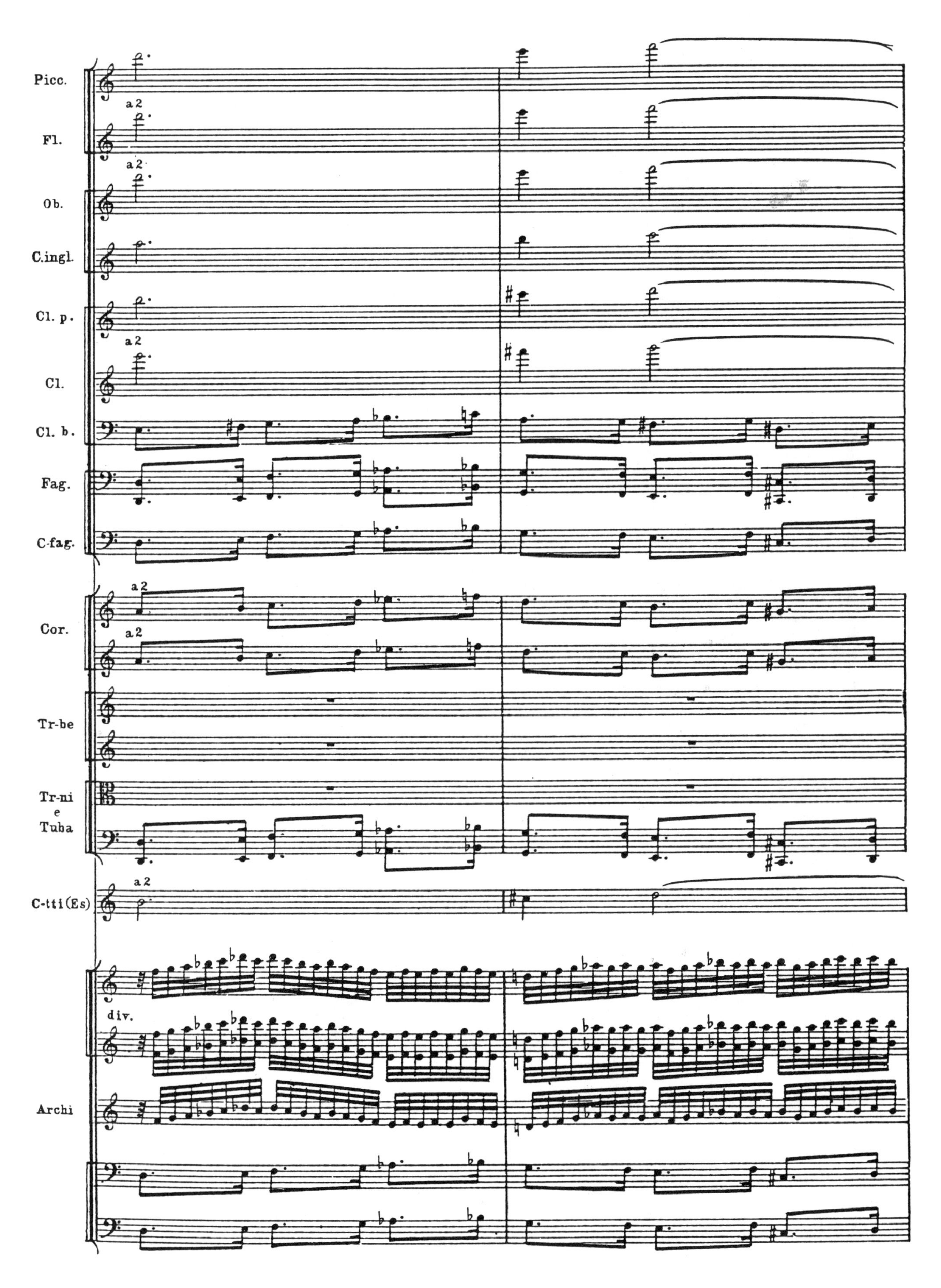

Picc.
a 2
Fl.
a 2
Ob.
C.ingl.
Cl. p.
a 2
Cl.
Cl. b.
Fag.
C-fag.
a 2
Cor.
a 2
Tr-be
Tr-ni
e
Tuba
a 2
C-tti (Es)
div.
Archi

Picc.
a 2
Fl.
a 2
Ob.
C.ingl.
Cl. p.
a 2
Cl.
Cl. b.
Fag.
C-fag.
a 2
Cor.
a 2
Tr-be
ff espr.
Tr-ni
e
Tuba
a 2
C-tti(Es)
unis.
Archi

Picc.
Fl.
a 2
Ob.
C.ingl.
Cl. p.
Cl.
Cl. b.
Fag.
C-fag.
Cor.
Tr-be
Tr-ni e Tuba
ff espr.
P-tti
ff
C-tti(Es)
div.
Archi

Variation 8

278
Picc.
Fl.
Ob.
C.ingl.
Cl. p.
Cl.
Cl. b.
Fag.
C-fag.
Cor.
Tr-be
Tr-ni e Tuba
Timp.
T - ro
P - tti
modo ordinario
C-tti (Es)
C-tti (B)
Tr-be (B)
Alti (Es)
Ten. (B)
Barit. (B)
Bassi
Archi
cresc.
a2
fff
80

Picc.
Fl.
Ob.
C.ingl.
Cl. p.
Cl.
Cl. b.
Fag.
C.fag.
Cor.
Tr-be
Tr-ni e Tuba
C-tti(Es)
C-tti(B)
Tr-be (B)
Alti (Es)
Ten. (B)
Barit. (B)
Bassi
Archi
a 2
f
fff
div.

rit.
Picc.
Fl.
a 2
Ob.
C.ingl.
Cl. p.
Cl.
Cl. b.
Fag.
C fag.
Cor.
fff
Tr-be
cresc.
Tr-ni e Tuba
Timp.
T-ro
p
C-tti(Es)
C-tti(B)
I
f
Tr-be(B)
Alti(Es)
Ten.(B)
Barit(B)
Bassi
unis.
Archi

Variation 9

279
a tempo
Picc.
Fl.
Ob.
C.ingl.
Cl. p.
Cl.
Cl. b.
Fag.
C-fag.
Cor.
Tr-be
Tr-ni e Tuba
Timp.
T-ro
P-tti
T-tam
C-tti(Es)
C-tti(B)
Tr-be(B)
Alti(Es)
Ten.(B)
Barit.(B)
Bassi
Archi
espr.

Picc.
a 2
Fl.
Ob.
C.ingl.
Cl. p.
Cl.
Cl. b.
a 2
Fag.
C-fag.
a 2
Cor.
ff
a 2
ff
mf
mf
a 2
Tr-be
ff
Tr-ni
e
Tuba
dim.
a 2
soli
mf
dim.
p
C-tti (B)
Alti (Es)
a 2
dim.
p
Ten. (B)
dim.
p
Barit. (B)
dim.
p
Bassi
dim.
Archi

Variation 10
280
Ob.
a 2
ff
dim.
Cl.
a 2
ff
dim.
Cl. b.
f
dim.
Fag.
a 2
f
dim.
C.fag.
f
dim.
Cor.
Tr-be
mf
mf
Tr-ni e Tuba
a 2
dim.
p
III
p
dim.
dim.
Arpe
f
dim.
8
280
solo
V-c.
ff espr.
dim.
altri
f
dim.
C-b.
f
dim.
100

Variation II

105

I
Cl.
Arpe
8
solo
V-c.
altri
C-b.
110
Arpe
8
V-c.
dim.
C-b.
115
CODA
Arpe
8
120
V-c.
p
dim.
pp
pp
C-b.
pp
pp
attacca

PART IV CHORAL MUSIC

• 22 •

Anton Webern (1883–1945)

Second Cantata, op. 31 (1941–43):
Fifth Movement ("Freundselig ist das Wort")

The Second Cantata is Webern's last completed composition. With its large instrumental and vocal forces, six movements, and length of about twenty-five minutes, it constitutes the most substantial of all his works.

Webern drew in this cantata upon six poems by his friend and confidante Hildegard Jone. The texts are not unified by narrative or theme, but they speak with great delicacy of several ideas that were embraced by Webern: love of nature, pantheism, and confidence in God's love.

The fifth movement was conceived by Webern, as he remarks in a letter to Jone, as an aria. Its central point occurs in measures 25–26, upon the words, "because it fell silent on the cross." After this passage, Webern tells Jone, "what went before is now repeated backwards."

The score of the fifth movement reproduced here is a piano reduction made by the composer in 1944. The original version uses a chamber orchestra in addition to soprano and bass soloists and mixed chorus.

TEXT

Blessed is the word, which, for our love, draws us to it. "Be not afraid, it is I"; be consoled through the darkness. It is in our midst when we are peaceful. For what can be in our midst other than the word? Because it fell silent on the cross we must pursue it; our living being follows Him with all the earnestness of bitterness. But when it sounds again in the morning, we who are called blissfully respond. Blessed is the word. And when you see that it sees everything in you, then you will know this: it will bring you more pain than death if a cloud of hostility—mother of tears—spreads itself between you and Him and brings coldness.

Bibliography

Music of the Twentieth Century, Chapter 7.

Kolneder, Walter. *Anton Webern: An Introduction to his Works*, pp. 158–62. Trans. Humphrey Searle. Berkeley and Los Angeles, 1968.

Moldenhauer, Hans, and Rosaleen Moldenhauer. *Anton von Webern: A Chronicle of his Life and Work*, pp. 573–79 and passim. New York, 1979.

Discography

The Complete Works of Anton Webern, vol. 1. Halina Lukomska, soprano; Barry McDaniel, baritone; John Aldis Choir; London Symphony Orchestra, Pierre Boulez, conductor. Columbia M4 35193 (1978).

Copyright 1951 by Universal Edition, Wien. Copyright renewed. All rights reserved. Used by permission of European American Music Distributors Corporation, sole U.S. agent for Universal Edition.

morendo
tempo
ich bin es;"
das mit-ten un-ter
trö - stet durch die Dun-kel - heit,
trö - stet durch die Dun-kel - heit,
trö - stet durch die Dun-kel - heit,
trö - stet durch die Dun-kel - heit,
9
rit. - - - tempo rit. - - tempo
uns ist,
wenn wir fried - lich sind.
wenn wir fried - lich sind.
wenn wir fried - lich sind.
wenn wir fried - lich sind.
13

ruhig fließend
Was kann denn an - dres mit - - ten un - ter
17
uns sein, als das Wort?
sehr getragen
molto f
Weil es am Kreuz ver-stumm-te
22
rit. - - - tempo
müs-sen wir ihm nach, in al - len Ernst der Bit-ter-nis ihn fol-get
27
espr. p
rit.
wieder ruhig fließend
un - ser Hauch. Doch wenn es wie-der
poco f
31
molto f

rit. - - - - tempo
auf - klingt in der Mor-gen-frü - he dann wen-den wir uns
espr.
poco f
36
rit. - - - tempo
al - le se - lig als Ge-ruf-ne um.
40
wieder sehr mäßig ♪ = ♩. [ca 56]
Und wenn du weißt, daß es um al-les
Freund - se - lig ist das Wort.
Freund - se - lig ist das Wort.
Freund - se - lig ist das Wort.
Freund - se - lig ist das Wort.
46
molto f

rit.
Dei - ne weiß.
dann kennst du es:
dann kennst du es:
dann kennst du es:
dann kennst du es:
49
tempo
drängend
rit.
dann tut's dir we-her als der Tod,
Feind - se-lig-keit:
wenn ei - ne Wol-ke
wenn ei - ne Wol-ke
wenn ei - ne Wol-ke
wenn ei - ne Wol-ke
51

tempo
leicht
p
sich zwi-schen dir und
pp
der Trä - nen Mut-ter
der Trä - nen Mut-ter
der Trä - nen Mut-ter
der Trä - nen Mut-ter
54
ihm
er-wei-tert
morendo
und die Käl - te schafft.
und die Käl - te schafft.
und die Käl - te schafft.
und die Käl - te schafft.
57
sf

• 23 •

Igor Stravinsky (1882–1971)

Mass (1944–48):
Credo

Stravinsky intended his Mass to be used in the Roman Catholic service of worship. It is a setting of the five texts of the Ordinary of the Mass traditionally employed in musical settings, and Stravinsky calls for a modest number of performers and relatively concise lengths to make it all the more utilitarian. Echoes of earlier styles of Mass compositions will be heard in different parts of the work: Renaissance polyphony in the Kyrie, medieval organum in the Gloria, chant in the Credo, and the baroque polychoral concerto in the Agnus Dei. The instrumentation of the work, which consists of ten brass and woodwind instruments in addition to the chorus, is reminiscent of the chamber wind ensembles favored by Stravinsky from the time of *Reynard* (1916) to the Piano Concerto (1924). The instrumentation also has precedents in Renaissance sacred music in which choral parts were often joined by wind instruments.

The Credo is the central and longest movement of the Mass. It is begun in the traditional manner of polyphonic Credos by an intonation in chant. The chorus then continues in a declamation in which rhythms, phrases, and cadences closely follow the sense and structure of the Latin words. The instruments add an unobtrusive support.

TEXT

I believe in one God, the Father Almighty, Maker of heaven and earth, of all things visible and invisible. All in one; Lord Jesus Christ, the only-begotten Son of God. And born of the Father before all ages: God of God, light of light, true God of true God, begotten, not made, consubstantial with the Father, by whom all things were made. Who for us men and for our salvation descended from heaven; and was incarnate by the Holy Ghost, of the Virgin Mary; and was made man. He was crucified also for us, suffered under Pontius Pilate, and was buried. And the third day He rose again, according to the Scriptures, and ascended into heaven. He sits at the right hand of the Father, and again He shall come with glory to judge the living and the dead. His kingdom shall have no end. And in the Holy Ghost, the Lord and giver of life, Who proceeds from the Father and the Son; Who together with the Father and the Son is adored and glorified; Who spoke by the prophets. And one, holy, Catholic and apostolic church. I confess one baptism for the remission of sins. And I await the resurrection of the dead and the life of the world to come. Amen.

Bibliography

Music of the Twentieth Century, Chapter 10.

Craft, Robert. "1949: Stravinsky's Mass: A Notebook." In *Igor Stravinsky*, pp. 201–206. Ed. Edwin Corle. New York, 1949.

Stravinsky, Igor, and Robert Craft. *Expositions and Developments*, pp. 76–77. Garden City, N.Y., 1962.

White, Eric Walter. *Stravinsky: The Composer and his Works*, pp. 446–50. 2d ed. Berkeley and Los Angeles, 1979.

Discography

The Saint Anthony Singers; members of the English Chamber Orchestra, Colin Davis, conductor. Editions de l'Oiseau-Lyre (1963).

Stravinsky Conducts. Gregg Smith Singers; Columbia Symphony Winds and Brass, Igor Stravinsky, conductor. Columbia MS 6992 (1967).

Chorus and Orchestra of the Belgrade Radio/Television, Borivoje Simié, conductor. Everest SDBR 3399 (1976).

English Bach Festival Chorus; members of the English Bach Festival Orchestra, Leonard Bernstein, conductor. Deutsche Grammophon 2530880 (1977).

© Copyright 1948 in U.S.A. by Boosey & Hawkes, Inc. Copyright for all countries. Reprinted by permission.

20
D.
Fi-li-um De—i u-ni—ge-ni-tum. Et ex Pa-tre na—tum......... an-te om-ni-a sae——cu—
A.
T.
Fi-li-um De—i u-ni—ge-ni-tum. Et ex Pa-tre na—tum......... an-te om-ni-a sae——cu—
B.
Ob. I. II
C. I.
I. II
Trb.
III
25
30
D.
—la. De-um de De-o, lu-men de lu-mi-ne, De—um ve—rum de... De-o
A.
T.
—la. De-um de De-o, lu-men de lu-mi-ne, De—um ve—rum de De-o
B.
Ob. I. II
C. I.
Fag. I. II
I. II
Trb.
III

35
40
D.
ve — ro. Ge-ni-tu-(u)m, non fac-tum, con-sub-stan-ti-a-lem Pa-tri: per quem om-ni — a
A.
T.
ve — ro. Ge-ni-tu-(u)m, non fac-tum, con-sub-stan-ti-a-lem Pa-tri: per quem om-ni — a
B.
Ob. I.II
a 2
C.I.
Fag. I.II
I
Trb.
III
45
50
fac-ta sunt. Qui pro-pter nos ho-mi — nes et pro-pter no-stram sa — lu-tem des — cen-
I.II

55
D.
—dit de coe–lis. Et in—— car–na–tus est de Spi–ri–tu Sanc–to ex Ma——— ri—a
A.
T.
—dit de coe–lis. Et in—— car–na–tus est de Spi–ri–tu Sanc–to ex Ma——— ri—a
B.
Ob. I. II
C. I.
I. II
Trb.
III
60
65
Orch. Interlude (mm. 66–70)
D.
Vir–gi—ne: Et ho—— mo fac–tus est.
A.
T.
Vir–gi—ne: Et ho—— mo fac–tus est.
B.
Ob. I. II
C. I.
Fag. I. II
Tr. I in Sib
I
Trb.
II
Trb.
III

C (mm. 71-101)
70
D.
A.
T.
B.
Cru-ci-fi-xus e-ti-am pro........ no——bis: sub
Ob. I.II
C.I.
I
Fag.
II
75
80
Pon-ti-o Pi——la-to pas-sus et se-pul——tus est. Et re-sur——re——xit
p leg.
Tr. in Sib
Trb.
II. III

85
D.
ter-ti-a di—e, sec-un-dum Scrip-tu——ras. Et as-cen—dit in coe——lum: se-det
A.
T.
ter-ti-a di—e, sec-un-dum Scrip-tu——ras. Et as-cen—dit in coe——lum: se-det
B.
Fag. I. II
I
Tr. in Sib
II
I
Trb.
II. III
90
95
D.
ad dex-te-ram Pa—tris. Et i—te—rum ven-tu-rus est cum glo-ri——a, ju-di——ca-re vi-vos
A.
T.
ad dex-te-ram Pa—tris. Et i—te—rum ven-tu-rus est cum glo-ri——a, ju-di——ca-re vi-vos
B.
Fag. I. II
I
Tr. in Sib
II
I
Trb.
II. III

A' (mm. 102-122)
100
D.
et mor-tu-os: cu-jus re-gni non e-rit fi-nis. Et in Spi-ri-tum
A.
T.
et mor-tu-os: cu-jus re-gni non e-rit fi-nis. Et in Spi-ri-tum
B.
Ob. I. II
C. I.
Fag. I. II
Tr. I. II in Sib
poco cresc.
I Trb. II. III
poco cresc.
105
110
Sanc-tum Do-mi-num et vi-vi-fi-can-tem: qui ex Pa-tre Fi-li-o-que
Sanc-tum Do-mi-num et vi-vi-fi-can-tem: qui ex Pa-tre Fi-li-o-que

115
D.
A.
T.
B.
pro—ce—dit, Qui cum Pa——tre et Fi—li—o si-mul a——do—ra——tur et con—
pro—ce—dit, Qui cum Pa——tre et Fi—li—o si-mul a——do—ra——tur et con—
Ob.I.II
C.I.
Fag.I.II
Tr.I.II in Sib
I
Trb.
II.III
120
D (mm.123-141)
——glo—ri—fi——ca—tur: qui lo——cu—tus est per Pro—phe—tas.
——glo—ri—fi——ca—tur: qui lo——cu—tus est per Pro—phe—tas.

125
130
poco più f
D.
Et u—nam...... sanc-tam ca—tho—li—cam et a—pos—to—li—cam Ec—cle—si—am.
A.
T.
B.
Ob. I. II
mf marc.
C. I.
Fag. I. II
mf
p
Tr. I. II in Sib
I Trb. II. III
135
p
Con-fi-te—or u-num bap-tis-ma in re—mis-si—o—nem pec—ca—to—rum. Et ex—

Codetta (mm. 142-147)
140
poco più f
145
D.
-spec-to re-sur-rec-ti-o-nem mor-tu-o-rum. Et vi-tam ven-tu-ri
A.
T.
-spec-to re-sur-rec-ti-o-nem mor-tu-o-rum. Et vi-tam ven-tu-ri
B.
Ob. I. II
mf marc.
C. I.
Fag. I. II
Tr. I. II in Sib
Trb. I II. III
Amen (mm. 148-153)
150
Poco meno mosso
sae-cu-li.
A-men, A-men.
Poco meno mosso

•24•

Edgard Varèse (1883–1965)

Octandre *(1923): First Movement*

Octandre is Varèse's work that most resembles traditional chamber music. The piece is divided into three movements, each in a clear and economical style. As the title suggests, it calls for an octet of instruments: flute, oboe, clarinet, bassoon, horn, trumpet, trombone, and string bass.

Compared to Varèse's other music, *Octandre* contains a large amount of motivic recurrence. The primary thematic idea is presented in the oboe at the beginning of the first movement. This line is based upon a descending chromatic scale, but its alternation of ninths, sevenths, and minor seconds gives it a distinctive shape. Varèse has the instruments play with great agility and in extremes of register. Typical of all of his works, the instruments are grouped into a kaleidoscope of changing colors.

Bibliography

Music of the Twentieth Century, Chapter 11.

Chou Wen-Chung. "Varèse: A Sketch of the Man and his Music." *Musical Quarterly*, 52 (1966), 151–70.

Vivier, Odile. *Varèse*, pp. 50–57. Paris, 1973.

Discography

Ensemble *Die Reihe*, Friedrich Cerha, conductor. Candide 31028; cassette CT 2303 (1970).

Contemporary Chamber Ensemble, Arthur Weisberg, conductor. Nonesuch H 71269 (1972).

The Varèse Album. Columbia Symphony Orchestra, Robert Craft, conductor. Columbia MG 31078 (1972).

Musica Nova, Siegfried Naumann, conductor. Caprice RIKS LP 34 (1975).

The Varèse Record. New York Wind Ensemble, Frederic Waldman, conductor. Finnadar SR 9018 (1977, recorded in 1950).

Stratford Ensemble, Raffi Armenian, conductor. Canadian Broadcasting System (1980).

Reprinted by courtesy of E. C. Kerby Ltd., Toronto. Revised and edited by Chou Wen-Chung.

Fl.
Hb.
Cl. Si♭
Bsn.
Cor
Tpt.
Trbn.
C.bsse
10
flatterzunge
fl.
sourd.

longue
Fl.
Hb.
Cl. Sib
Bsn.
Cor
Tpt.
Trbn.
C.bsse
fl.
sourd.
16
cuivrez

Fl.
Hb.
Cl. Sib
Bsn.
Cor
Tpt.
Trbn.
C.bsse
ouvert
sans sourd.
sans sourd.
19 Lourd et sauvage (♩ = 56)
bouché
cuivrez
sons réels
sifflant

22
Tempo I (♩= 63-66)
Fl.
Hb.
Cl. Si♭
Bsn.
Cor
ouvert
molto
Tpt.
molto
Trbn.
molto
C.bsse
Pos. nat.
molto
arco
pizz.
arco
pizz.
arco
sub. mp
sub. p
sub. p
p sub.
p sub.
sub. p

25
rall.
très scandé
très déclamé
Fl.
Hb.
Cl.Sib
Bsn.
Cor
Tpt.
Trbn.
C.bsse
morendo
rallentando molto
molto
sempre ff

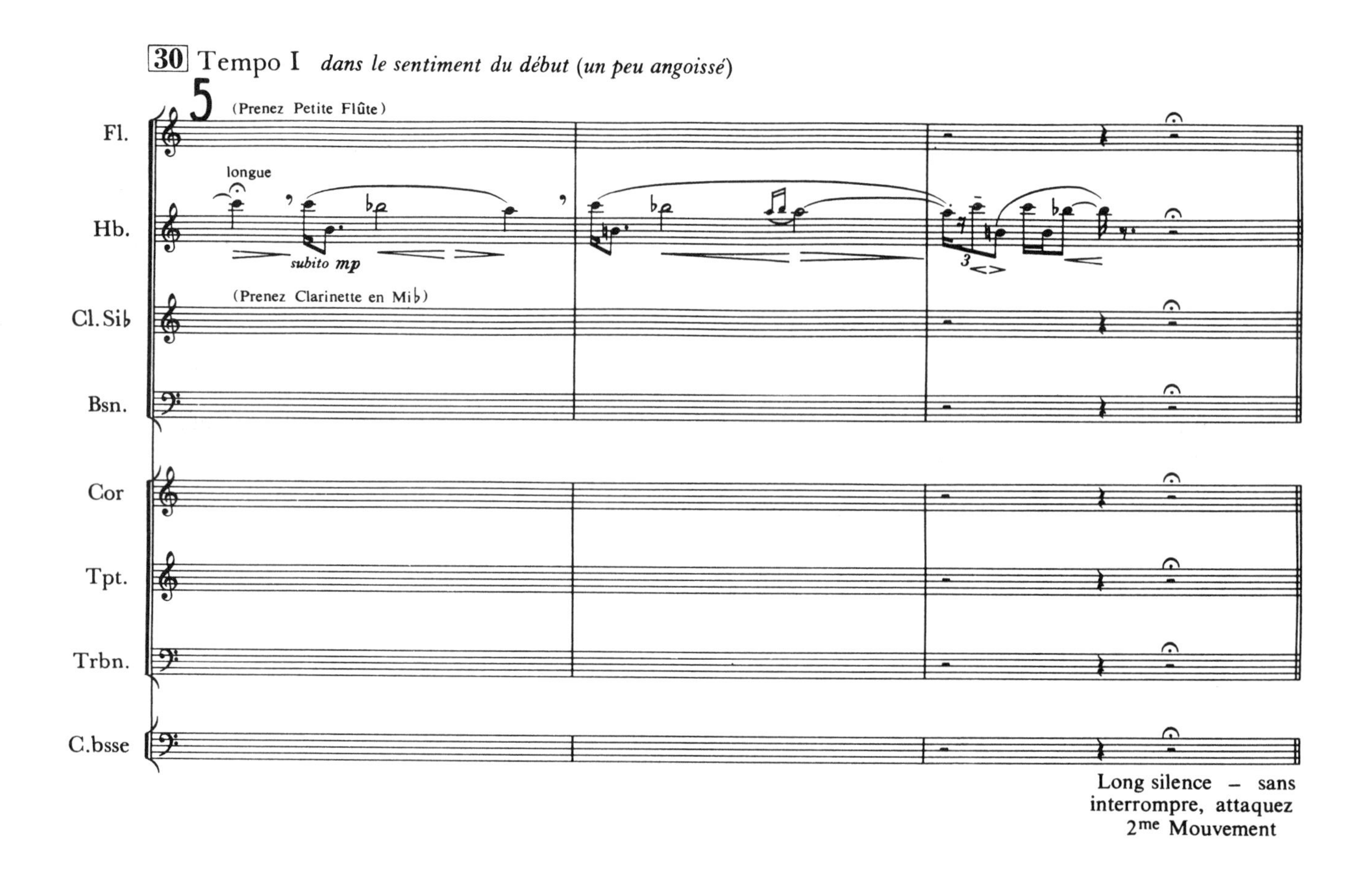
30 Tempo I dans le sentiment du début (un peu angoissé)
5
(Prenez Petite Flûte)
Fl.
longue
Hb.
subito mp
3
(Prenez Clarinette en Mi♭)
Cl. Si♭
Bsn.
Cor
Tpt.
Trbn.
C.bsse
Long silence – sans interrompre, attaquez 2me Mouvement

• 25 •

Arnold Schoenberg (1874–1951)

Fourth String Quartet, op. 37 (1936): First Movement (Allegro Molto; Energico)

Schoenberg composed his String Quartets nos. 3 and 4 upon receiving commissions from Elizabeth Sprague Coolidge—America's greatest patron of twentieth-century chamber music. The Fourth Quartet was written in 1936, shortly after Schoenberg moved to the Los Angeles area, where he taught at the University of Southern California and the University of California, Los Angeles.

The Fourth Quartet is one of his most accessible pieces in the twelve-tone idiom. It has a clarity of texture, diversity of color, and directness of rhythm that are less evident in his earlier quartets. The first movement invites comparison with traditional sonata form, although Schoenberg himself did not describe it in this way. In a brief analysis written in 1949 for record liner and program notes, he states that some themes recur "as landmarks or guides in a complicated organization where recognition is hindered by continual transformation." He points to the line in the first violin in measures 1–6 as the main theme, which is recapitulated prominently in measures 165 and following and again at measure 239. The theme in the first violin at measure 27 functions as a connective, transition, or element of contrast. The main subsidiary theme begins at measure 66.

Bibliography

Music of the Twentieth Century, Chapters 4 and 7.

Gradenwitz, Peter. "The Idiom and Development in Schoenberg's Quartets." *Music and Letters*, 26 (1945), 123–42.

Rufer, Josef. *Composition with Twelve Notes Related Only to One Another*, pp. 140–53. Trans. Humphrey Searle. London, 1954.

Schoenberg, Arnold. "Bemerkungen zu den vier Streichquartetten." In *Arnold Schönberg Gesammelte Schriften*, vol. 1, pp. 430–35. Ed. Ivan Vojtěch. N.p., 1976.

Discography

LaSalle Quartet. Deutsche Grammophon 2720029 (1972).

Schoenberg: The Five String Quartets. Juilliard Quartet. Columbia M3-34581 (1977).

Used by arrangement with G. Schirmer, Inc.

12
13
(G)
14
15
fp
f
fp
ff
sf
(C)
16
17
18
19
pp dolce
p dolce
20
21
22
sfp
f
sff

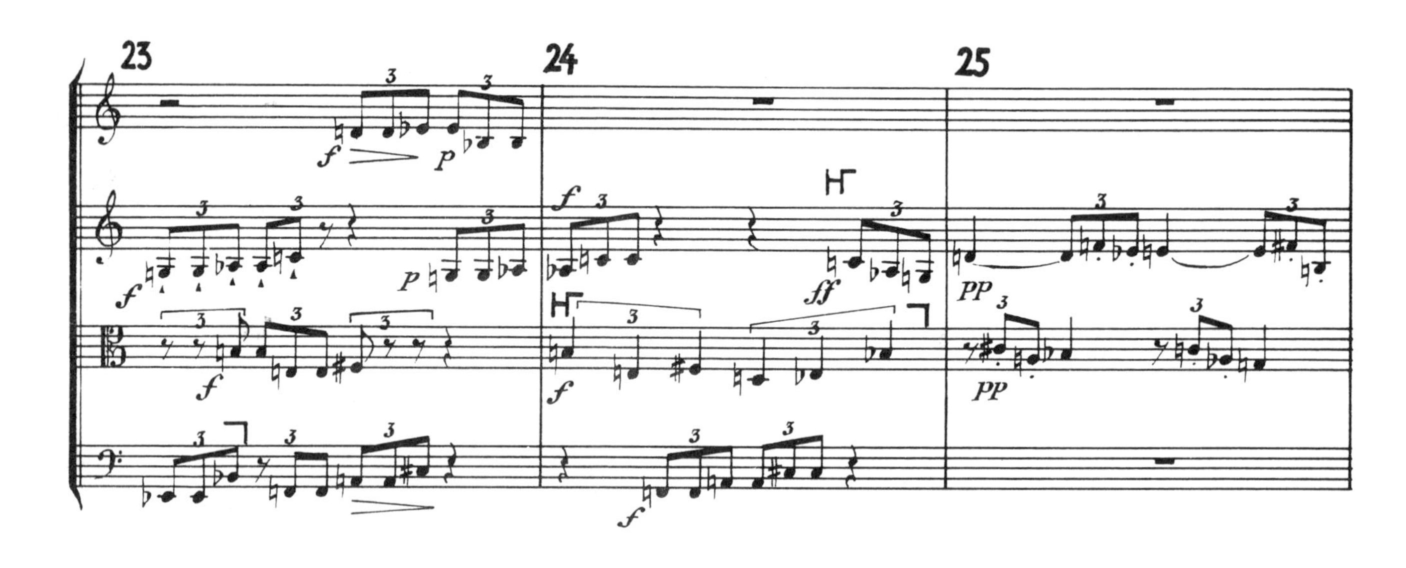
23
24
25
f
p
ff
pp

26
27
28
p dolce
pizz
p

29
30
31
cresc
arco
f
ff

p dolce

41
42
43
fp
p
44
45
46
impetuoso
f
47
48
49
ff
pizz

50
51
52
ff
p
pizz
arco
ff
fp
f
pizz
arco
ff
fp
f
arco
53
54
55
fp
p
fp
p
f
p
f
56
57
58
f
ff

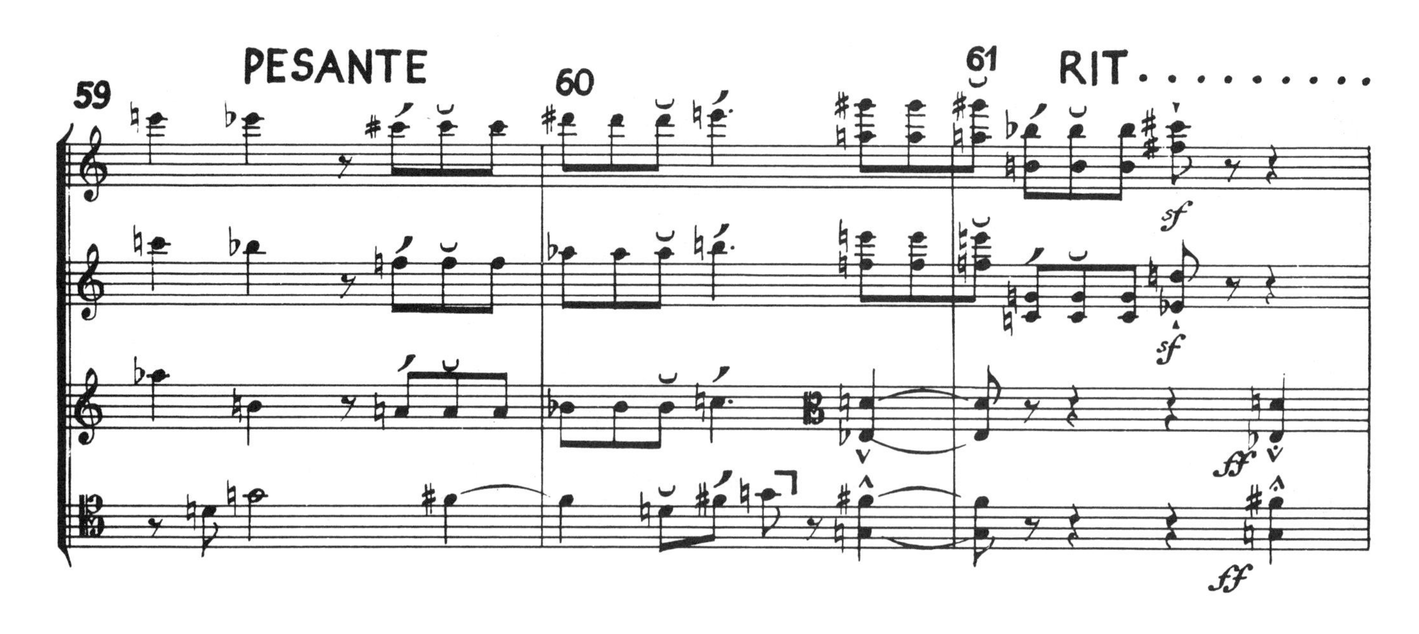
PESANTE
RIT
59
60
61
sf
ff

POCO MENO MOSSO
MOLTO RIT
62
63
64
p
pizz
arco
sul ponticello
sfpp

A TEMPO, MA POCO TRANQUILLO

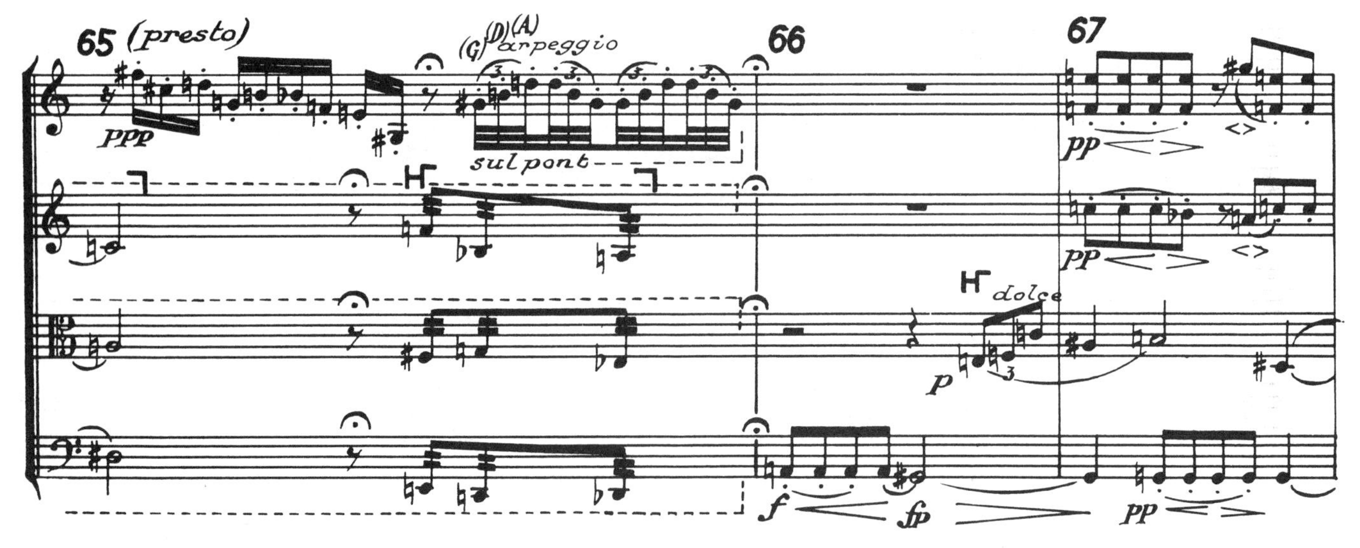
65 (presto)
arpeggio
sul pont
66
67
dolce
ppp
pp
p
f
fp

68
69
70
mf
mf
pp
pp
mf
pp
71
72
73
pp dolce
pizz
ppp
pizz
pp
arco
pp dolce
74
75
76
sempre pp
arco
pizz

77
78
(D)
(G)
(D)
79
pizz
pp
f
p
80
81
arco
pizz
arco
arco
ff
82
83
84

85
86
87
88
pp
pp
pp
pp
ff
ff
ff
ff
ff
ff
ff
ff

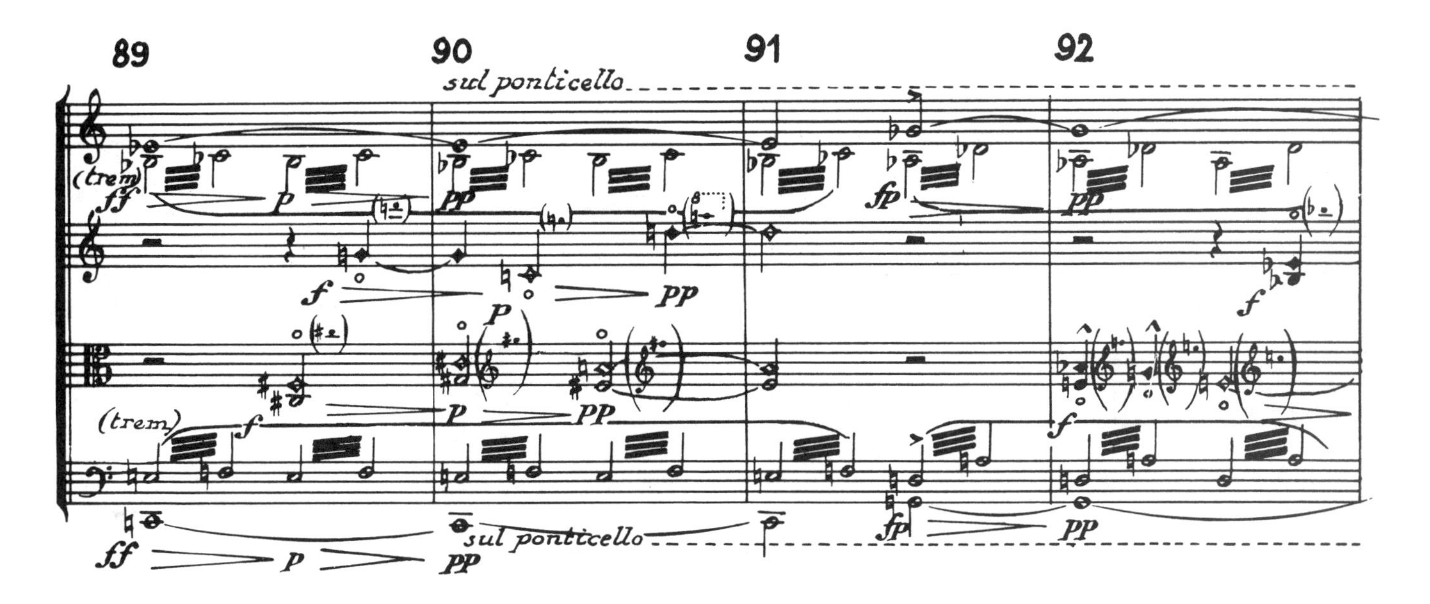
89
90
91
92
sul ponticello
(trem)
ff
p
pp
fp
pp
f
pp
f
p
(trem)
f
p
pp
f
ff
p
pp
sul ponticello
fp
pp

TEMPO Imo
93
94
95
96
H
H
H
ff
ff
ff
sf
ff
sf
ff

97
98
99
(G)
ff
sf
100
101
103
104
105
pp
f
3

106
107
108
ff
ponticello
(trem)
fpp
p
(D)
(G)
f
109
110
111
112
113
114
3

115
116
117
mf
f
f
f
impetuoso
118
119
120
121
122
123
mf
f
impetuoso
mf
mf

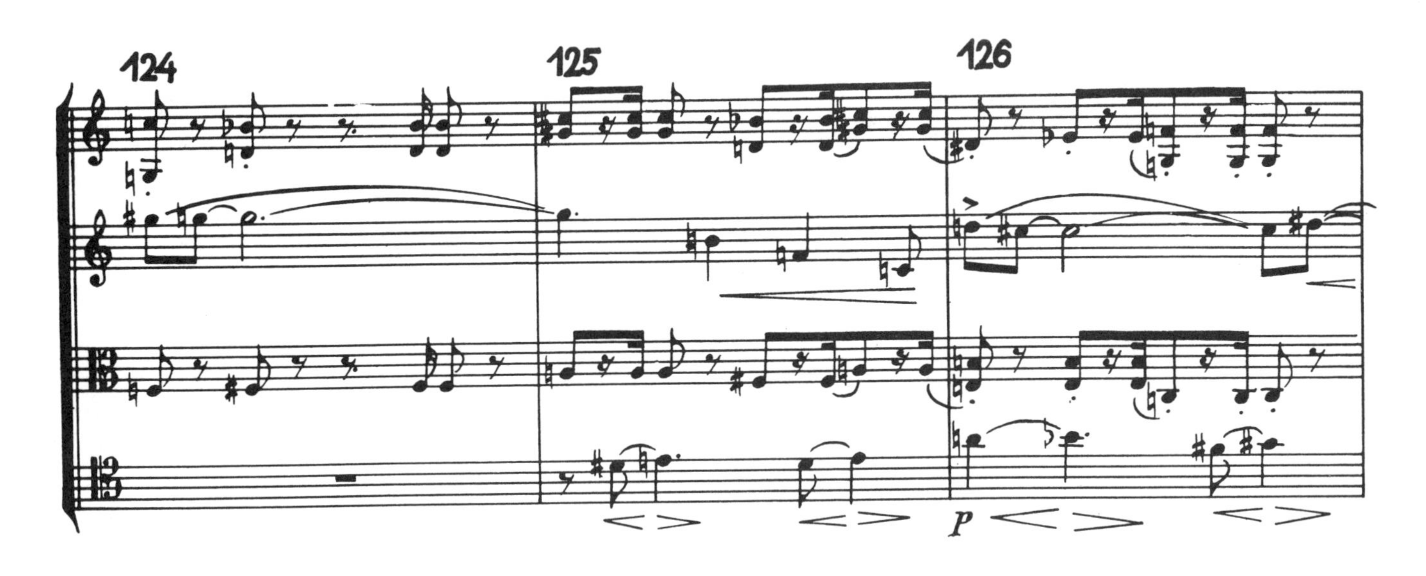
124
125
126
p

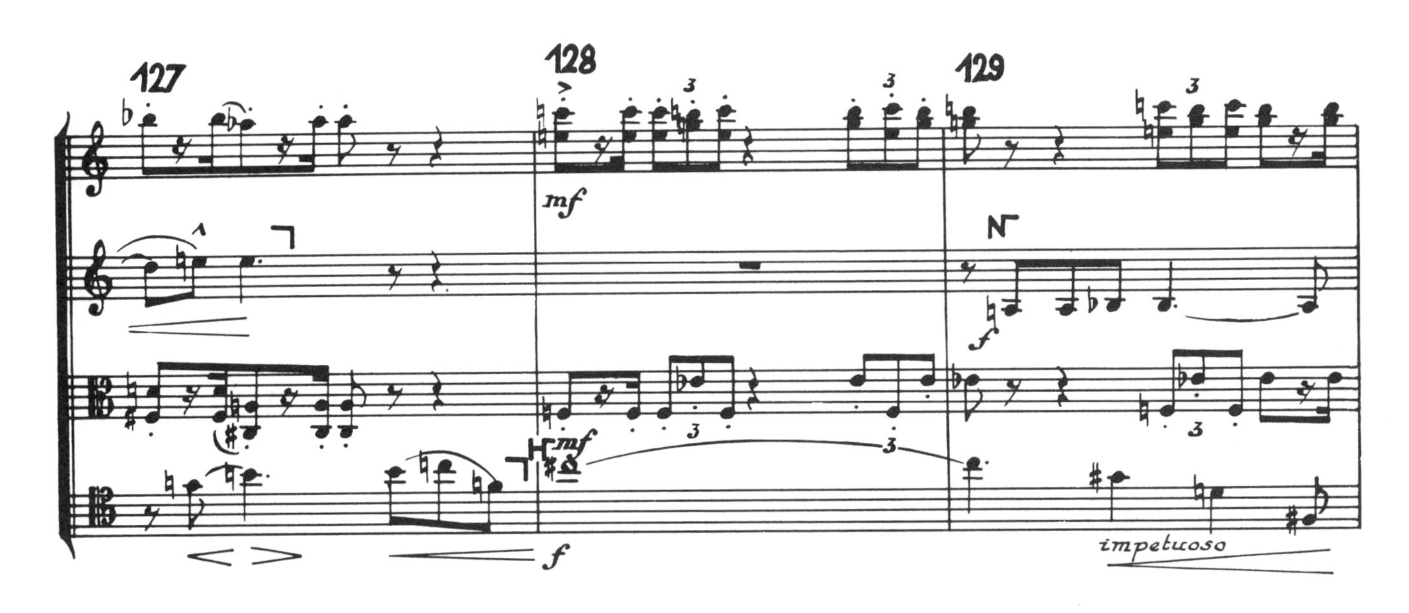
127
128
129
mf
f
impetuoso

130
131
132

133
134
135
f impetuoso
(G)
(A)
136
137
138
f martellato
139
(e)
140
141

142
143
144
PP
P
145
146
147
dolce
fp
f
148
149
150
151

POCO A POCO ACCELERANDO
152
153
154
155
156
157
158
159
160

161
162
163
TEMPO Imo
164
RIT
165
166
(G)
ff
pizz
167
168
169
fp
f

170
171
172
arco
173
174
175
RIT
176
PESANTE
177
POCO MOSSO
178

179
180
181
182
183
184
185
186
p
f
fp
fp
p
f
f
f

UN POCO TRANQUILLO
187
188
189
p dolce
p
pp
mf
190
191
192
193
194
195
pp

196
197
198
PP
P

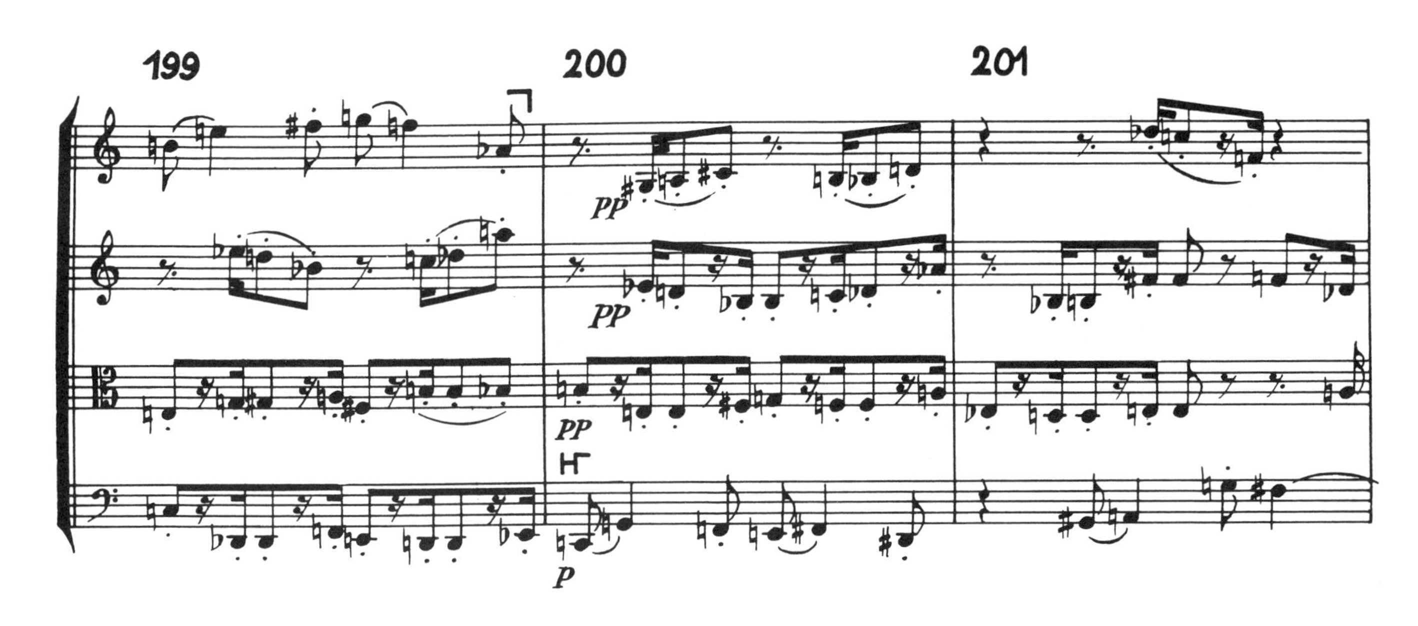
199
200
201
PP
P

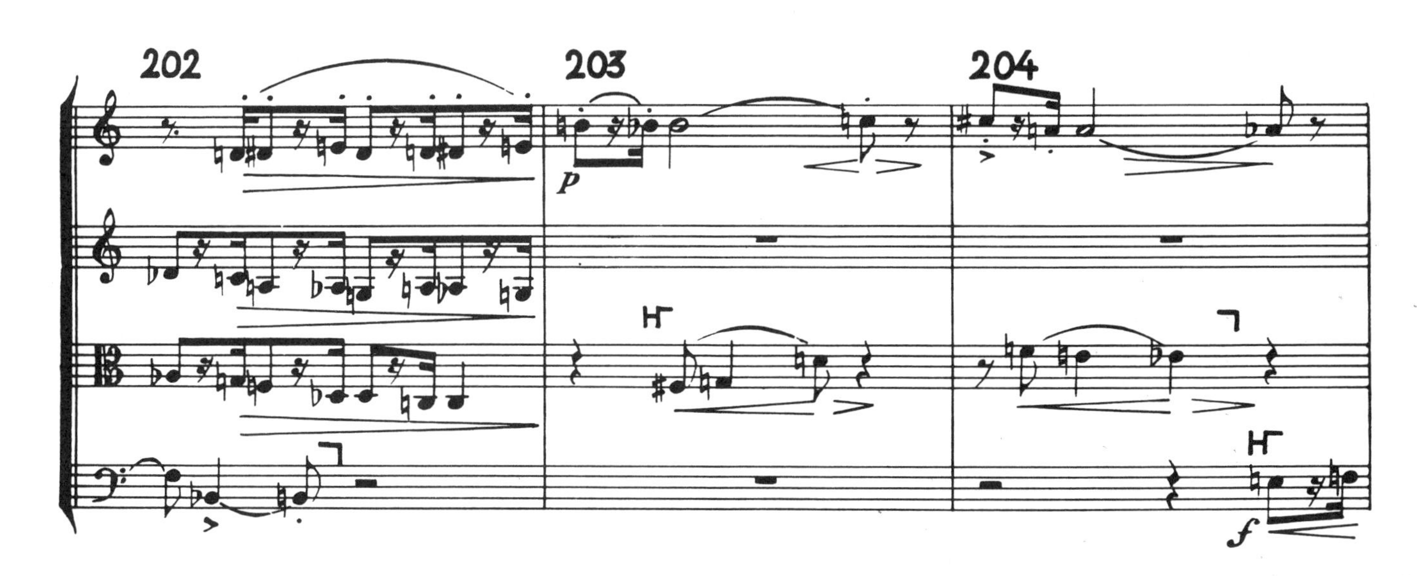
202
203
204
P
f

205
p
206
f
f
f
f
207
mf
f
sfmf
sfmf
208
mf
ff
ff
209
f
mf
mf
210
ff
ff
211
212
f
f
sf
f
sf
213
sf
sf
sf
sf
sf
sf
ff
ff

214
215
216

217
218
219
sempre ff
sempre ff
sempre ff
sempre ff

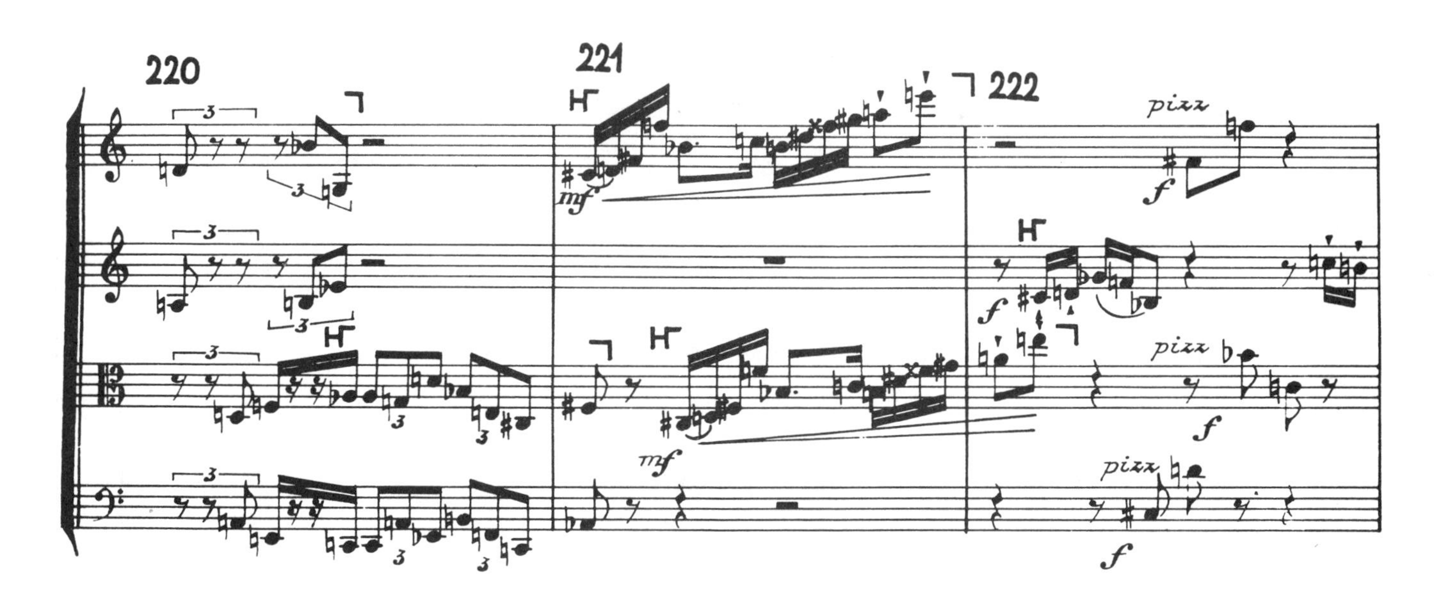
220
221
222
mf
mf
pizz
pizz
pizz
f
f
f
f

223
224
225
arco
arco
arco
mf
f
226
227
p
f
228
229

230
231
232
pizz
pizz

233
234
235
arco
arco
p
p
p
pizz
f

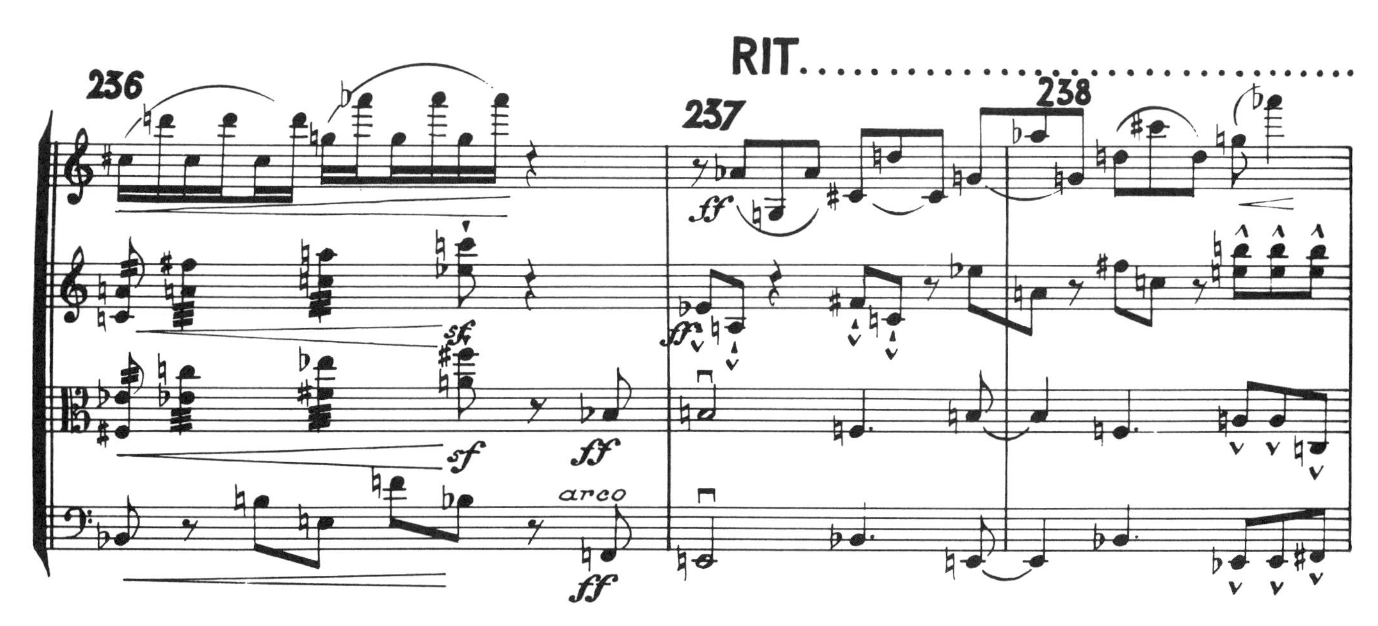
RIT.
236
237
238
ff
ff
sf
sf
ff
arco
ff

POCO MENO MOSSO ♩ = 108
239
240
241
242
243
244
245
mf
ff
f
sf

246
247

248
249
250
ff
f
mf

251
252
253
mf
f
p

POCO A POCO CALANDO
254
255
256
mf
p
mf
p
mf
p
mf
p
p
p
p

RIT
POCO MENO MOSSO
257
258
259
f
pp
f
f
p
pp
f
pp
3

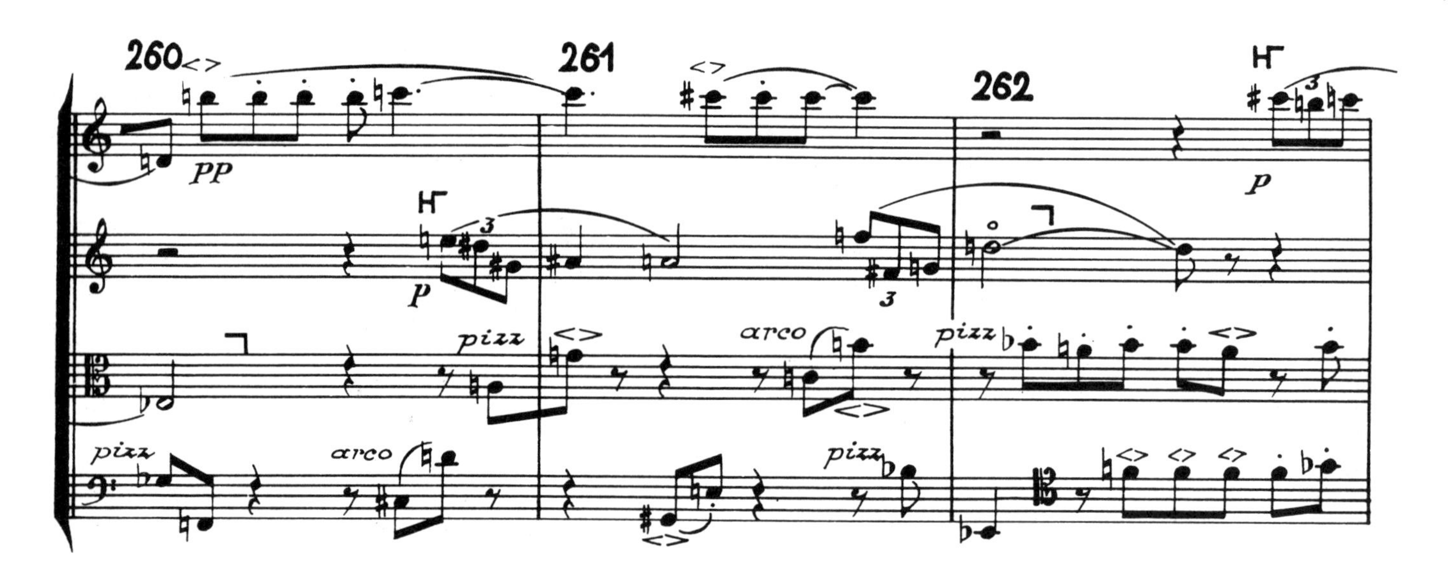
260
261
262
pp
p
p
pizz
arco
pizz
pizz
arco
pizz
3

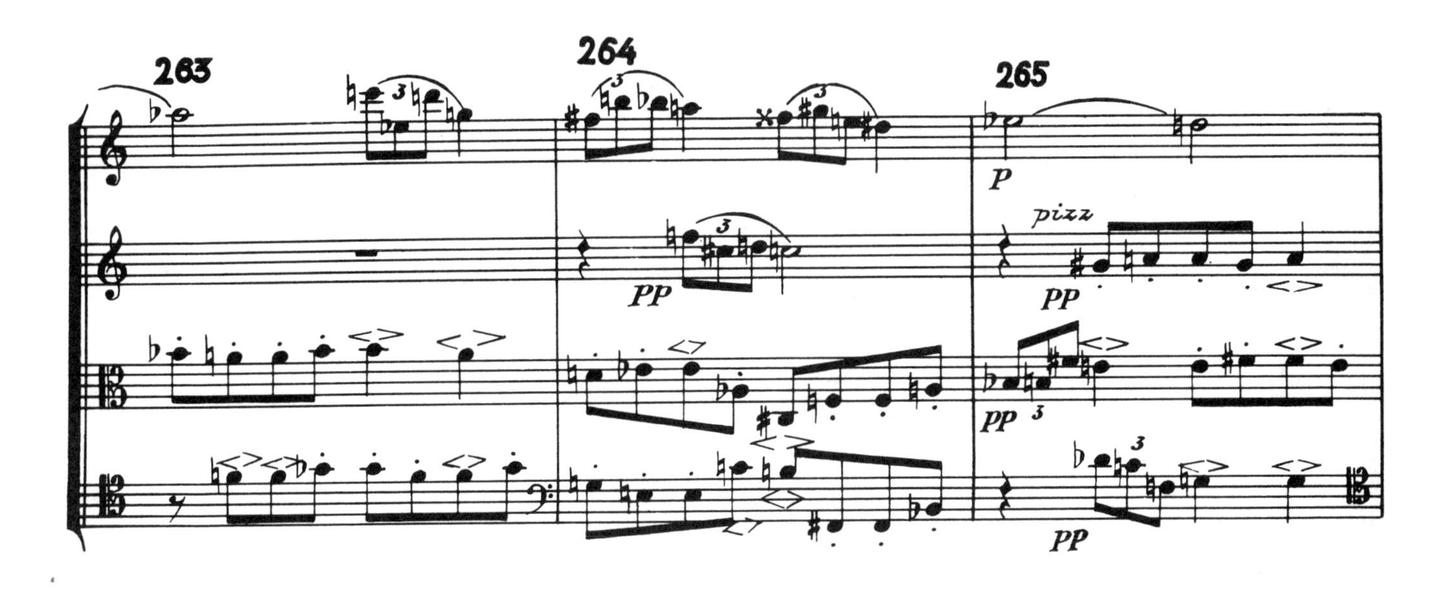
263
264
265
p
pizz
pp
pp
pp
pp
pp

266
267
268
pp
p
pp
pp
p
pp
pp
p
pp
pp
p
pp

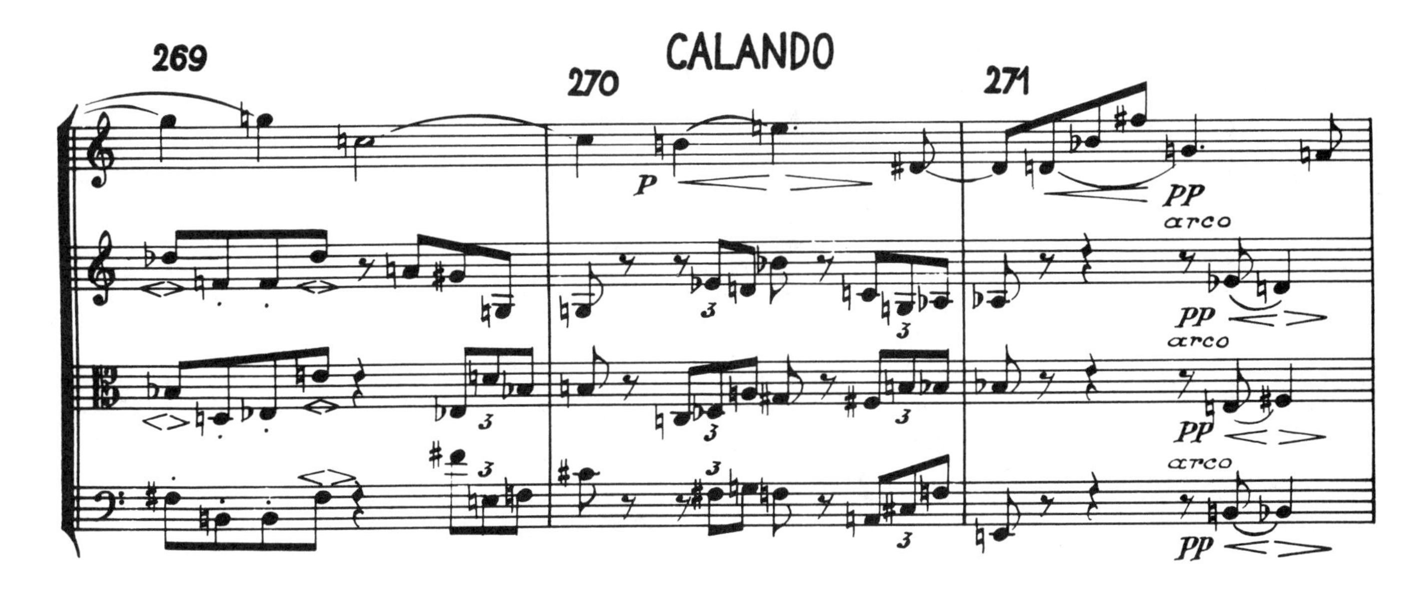
269
CALANDO
270
271
p
pp
arco
pp
arco
pp
arco
pp

TEMPO Imo
272
273
274
275
ff
f
276
277
278
279
fff
PESANTE
280
281
282
283
284

• 26 •

Karlheinz Stockhausen (1928-)

Kreuzspiel *(1951, revised 1959): Introduction and First Section*

Kreuzspiel (*Cross Play*) was Stockhausen's first essay in total or integral serialism: a compositional method in which the order of occurrences in several dimensions of a work are controlled or coordinated by predetermined series. In *Kreuzspiel*, pitch classes, registers, durations, and dynamics are thus organized and integrated.

Kreuzspiel is in three connected sections with a thirteen-measure introduction. The introduction and first section are divided into subsections, each of six and one-half measures. Pitches, durations, and dynamics in the first section (mm. 14–91) undergo a crossing, which is suggested by the title of the work. At the beginning of this section, for example, the piano states six pitch classes in the high register (E♭ D E G A A♭) and the other six in the low register. These pitch classes then pass into all registers, and they are taken increasingly by the woodwinds. Finally, they return to the piano with registers exchanged. Similarly, durations and dynamics "cross" from a state of diversity to one of regularity (e.g., the steady crescendo and accelerando in the woodblocks in mm. 46–53) and then return to diversity at the end of the section.

By Stockhausen's admission, *Kreuzspiel* is indebted in its integration of parameters and quasi-pointillistic texture to the piano étude "Mode de valeurs et d'intensités" by Olivier Messiaen and in its cruciform plan to the Sonata for Two Pianos by Karel Goeyvaerts. *Kreuzspiel* was revised in minor details for a performance at Darmstadt in 1959 and for its subsequent publication.

Bibliography

Music of the Twentieth Century, Chapter 12.

Keller, Max Eugen. "Gehörte und komponierte Struktur in Stockhausens 'Kreuzspiel,'" *Melos*, 39 (1972), 10–18.

Maconie, Robin. *The Works of Stockhausen*, pp. 21–27. London and Boston, 1976.

Stenzl, Jurg. "Karlheinz Stockhausen's *Kreuzspiel* (1951)." *Zeitschrift für Musiktheorie*, 3/1 (1972), 35–42.

Stockhausen, Karlheinz. "*Kreuzspiel* (1951)." In *Texte zu eigenen Werken*, vol. 2, pp. 11–12. Schauberg, 1964.

Toop, Richard. "Messiaen/Goeyvaerts, Fano/Stockhausen, Boulez." *Perspectives of New Music*, 13 (1974), 141–69.

Discography

London Sinfonietta. Deutsche Grammophon 2530443 (1974).

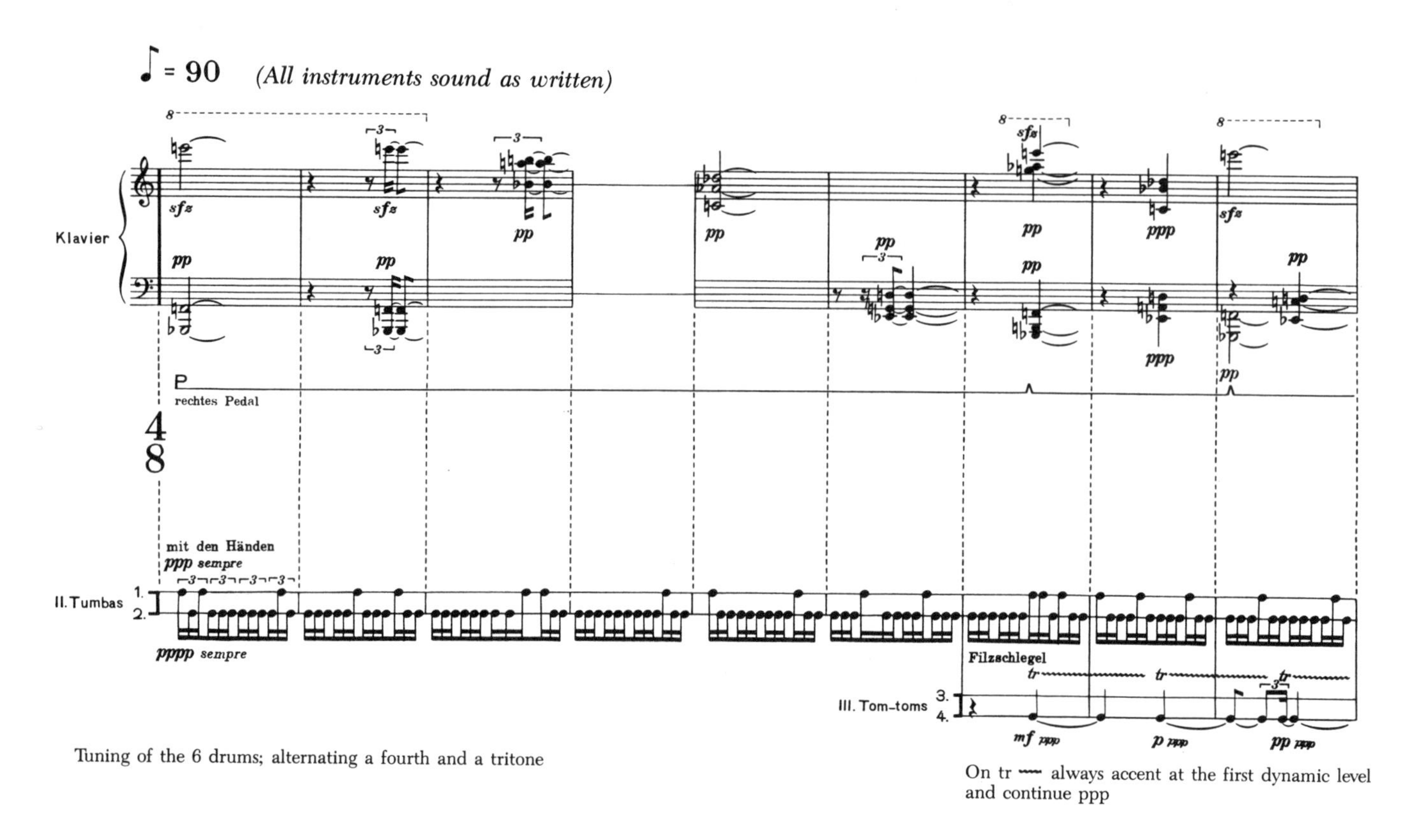

Tuning of the 6 drums; alternating a fourth and a tritone

On tr ~~~ always accent at the first dynamic level and continue ppp

①Durations without tr: at the conclusion of the value, damp the head with the hand

②On [notation] do not release the stick from the head

© Copyright 1960 by Universal Edition (London) Ltd., London. All rights reserved. Used by permission of European American Music Distributors Corporation, sole U.S. agent for Universal Edition.

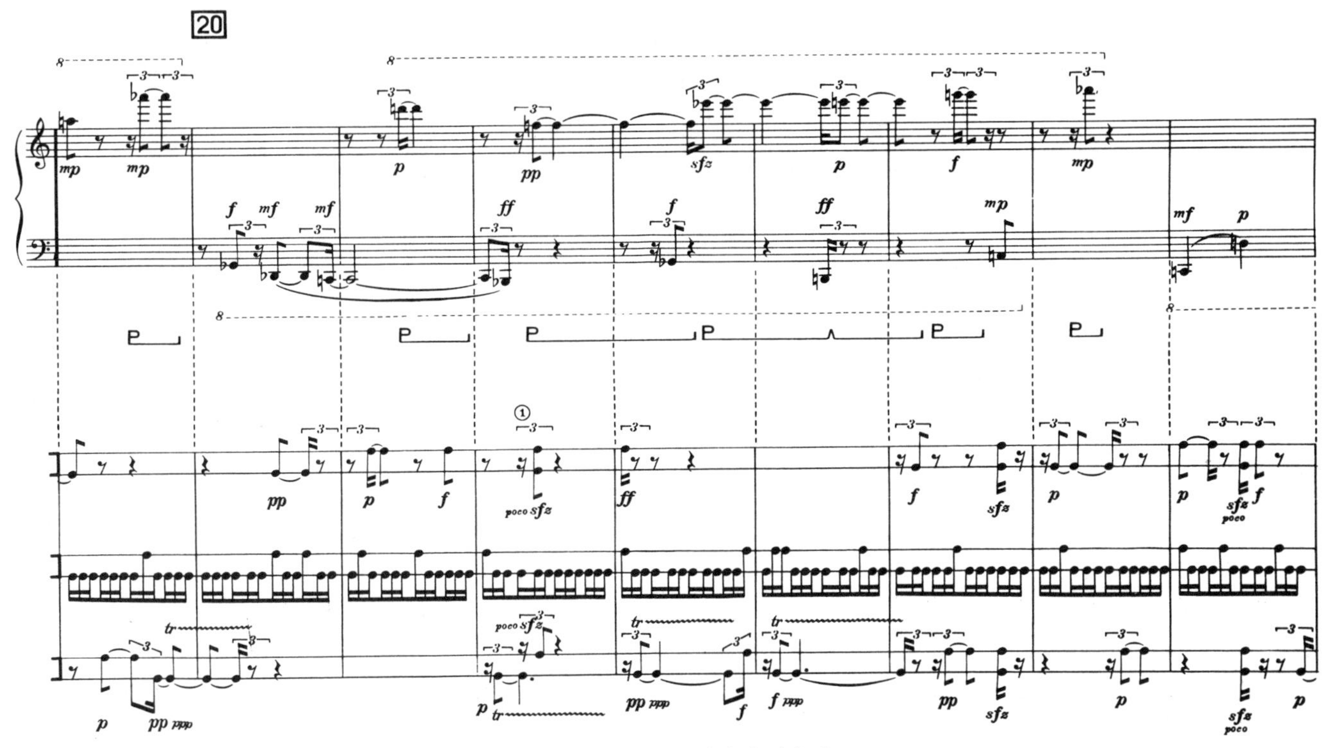

① sfz, (sfz) = strike the head and the rim at the same time with the soft tip and shaft of the beater.

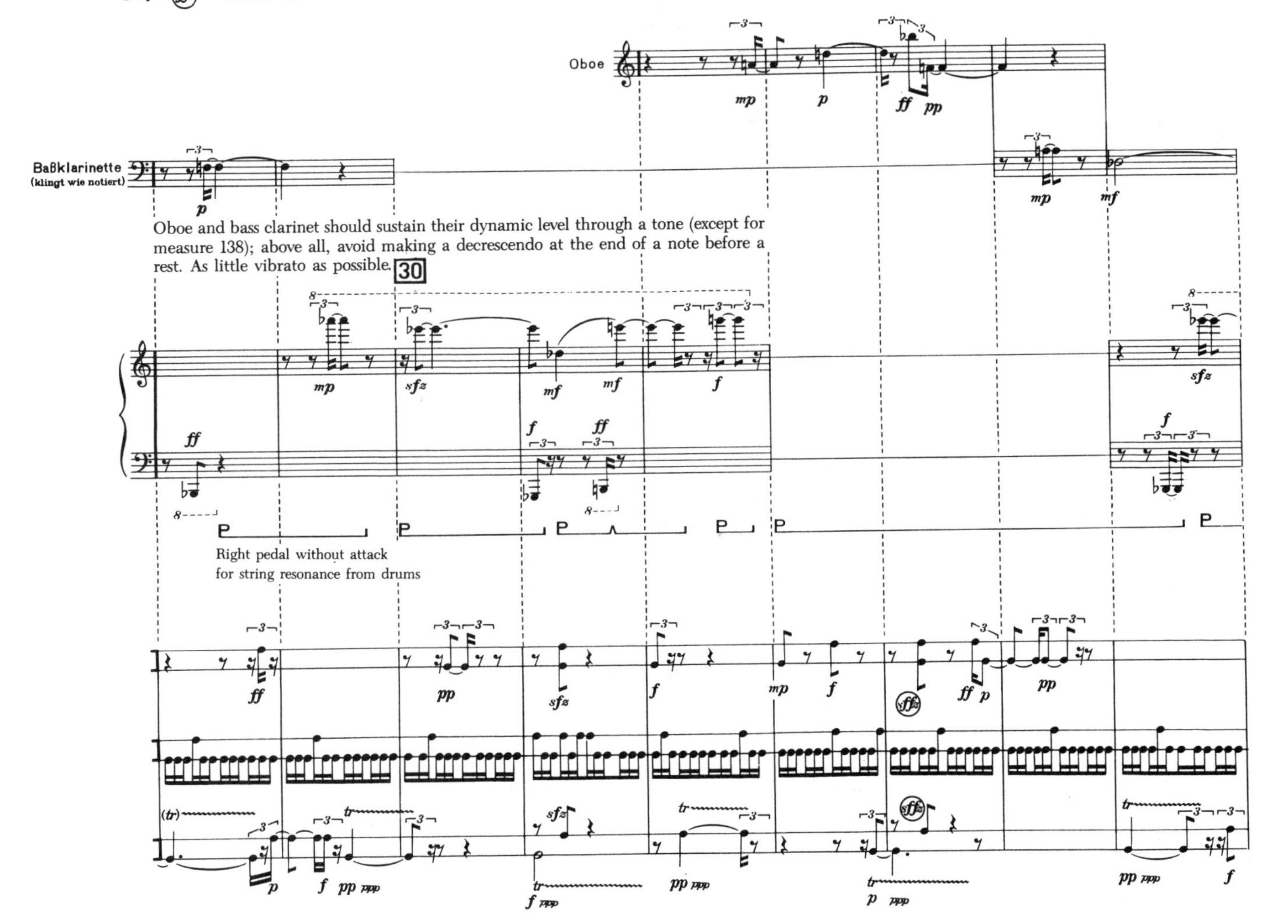

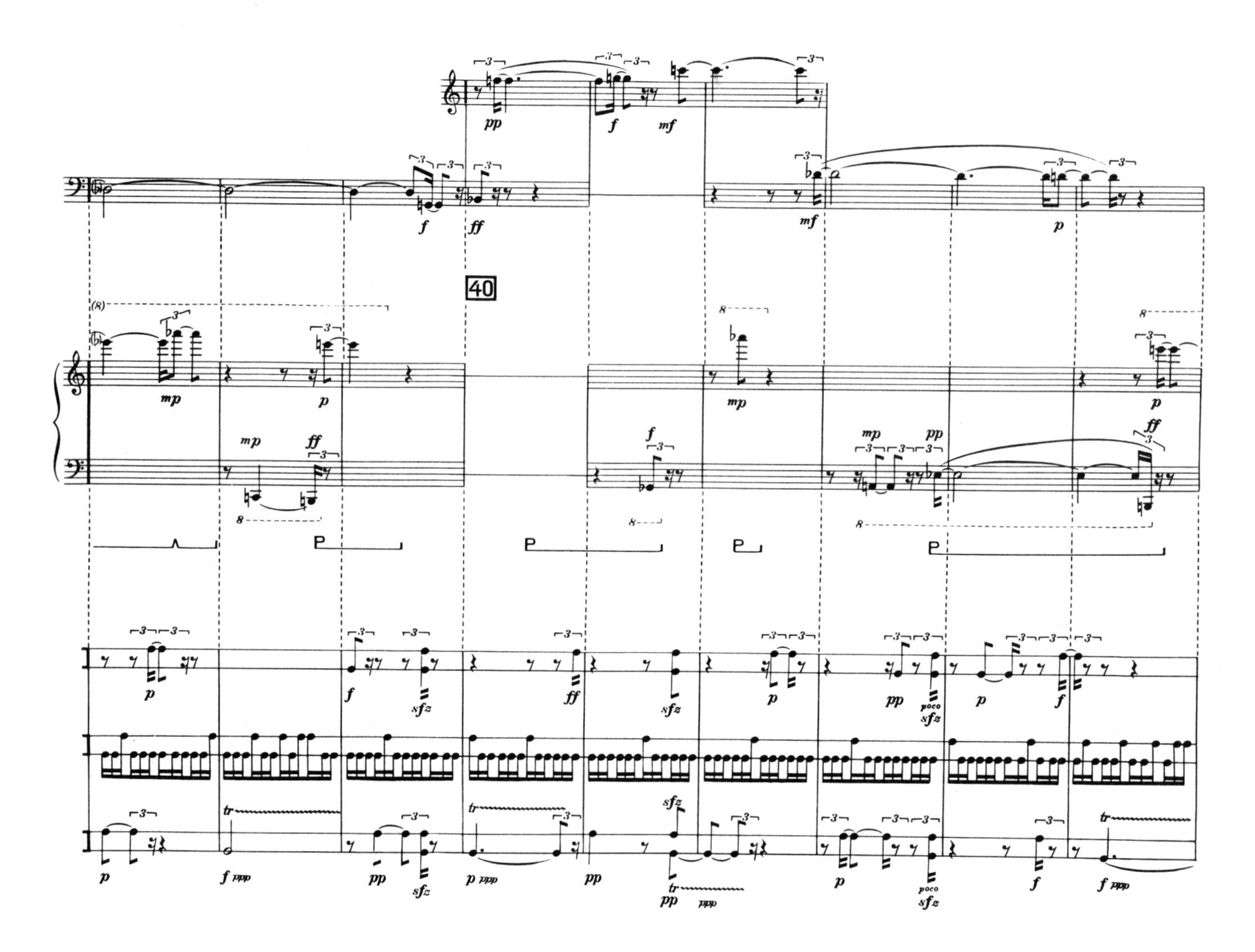
40
pp
f
mf
ff
mp
p
sfz
poco sfz
fppp
pppp
tr
pp ppp
8
(8)

50
Woodblock
Play wood block with right hand
poco
sempre

60

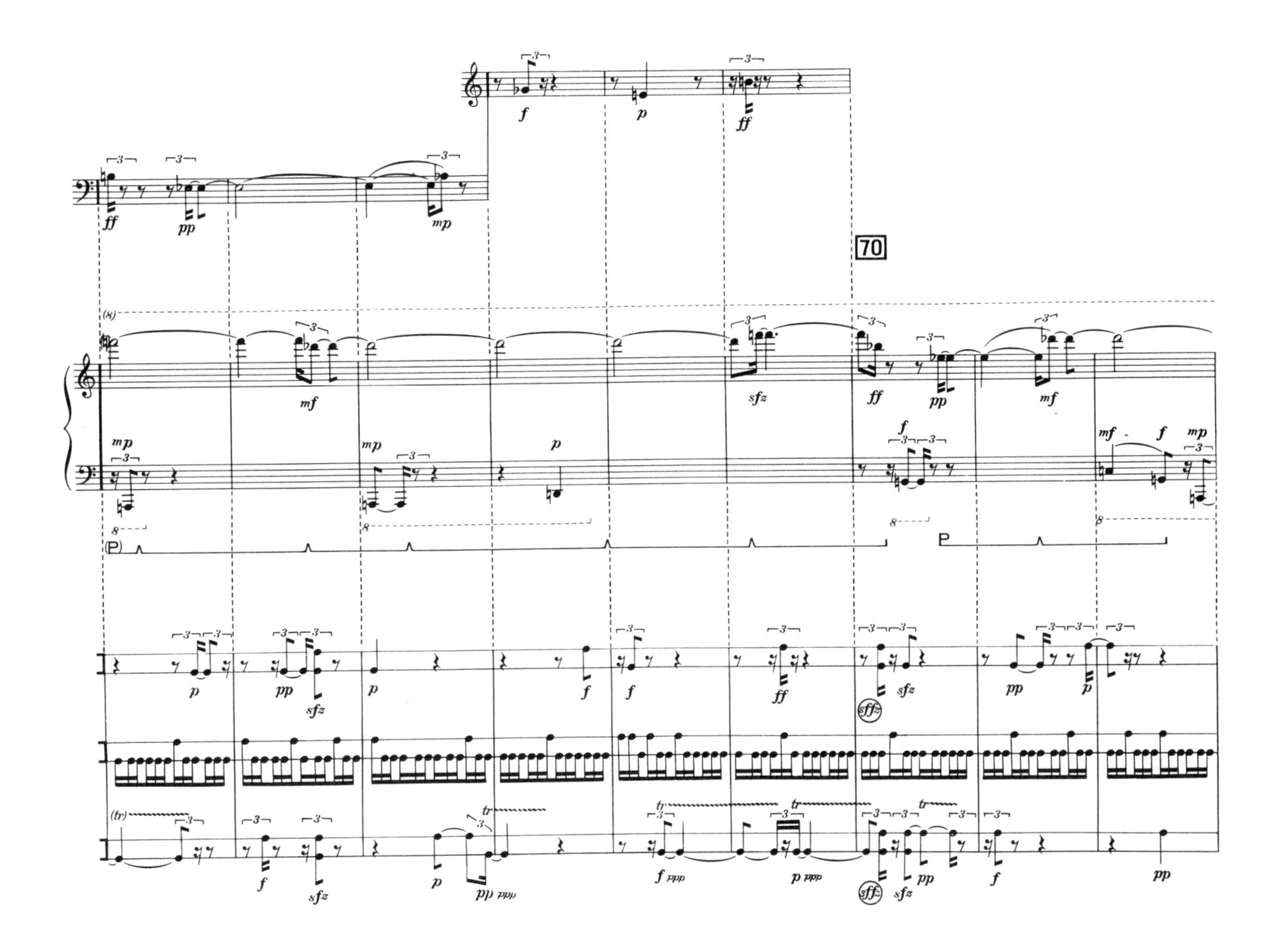
70
P

80
P
P

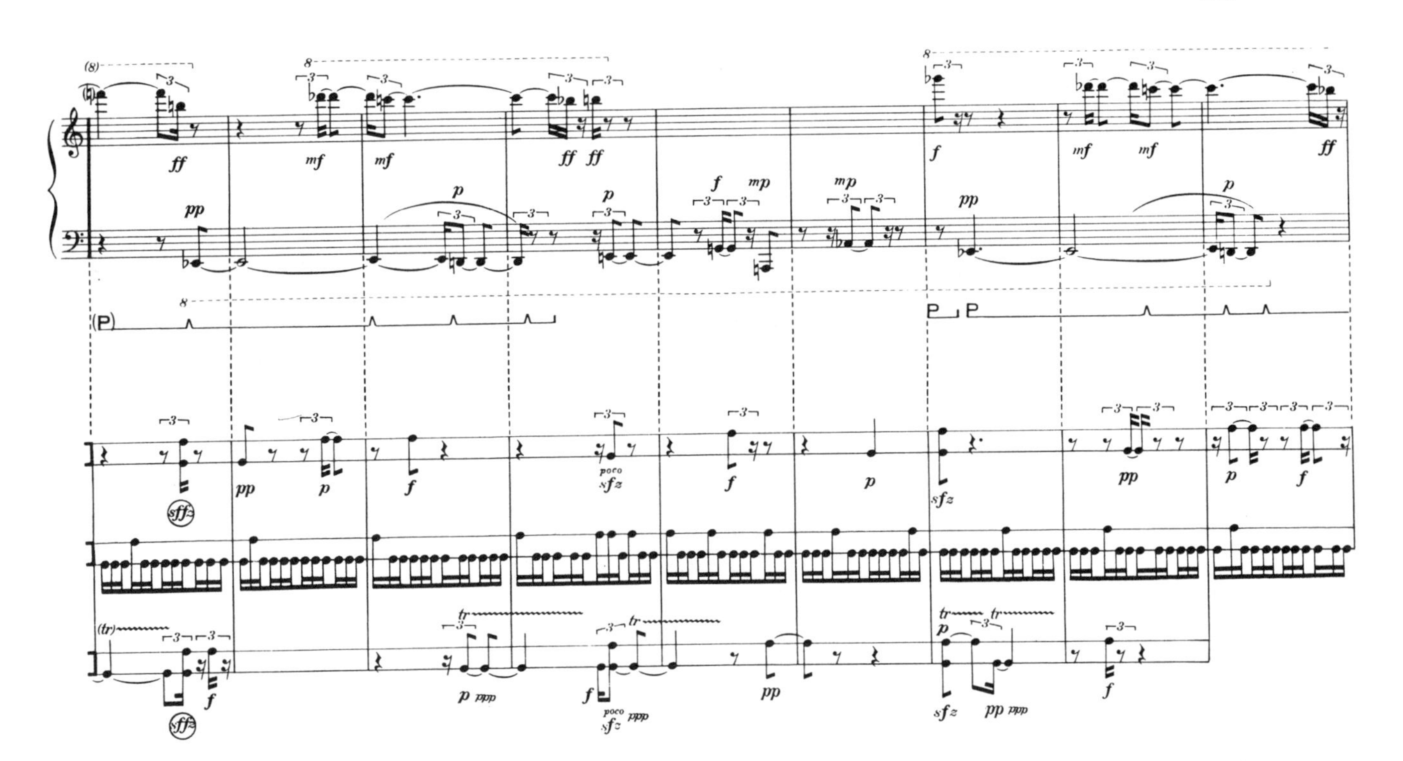

2′52″ ♩ = 90

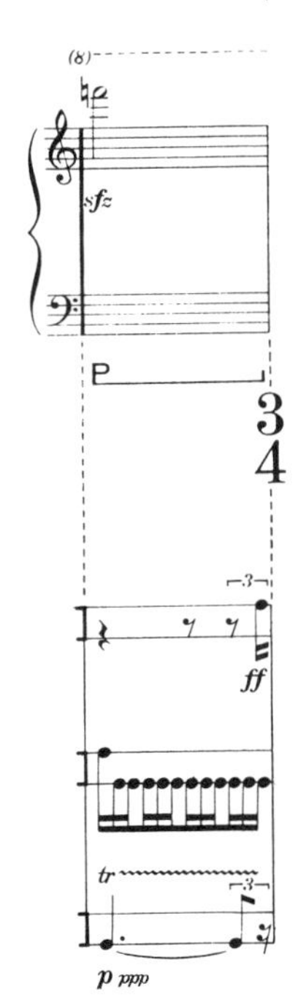

• 27 •

George Crumb (1929–)

Black Angels *(1970):*
Sections 6 and 7

Crumb's *Black Angels* for amplified string quartet is a symbolic and eclectic study in sound that represents the voyage of a soul through good and evil. The work consists of thirteen sections or "images," which are arranged symmetrically and articulated at the beginning, middle, and end by passages called threnodies. As symbolic references to good and evil, there is a pervasive use of the numbers 7 and 13. These are expressed by the lengths of phrases, repetitions of pitches or figures, durations, numbers of semitones between notes of important chords, and similar devices.

In the sixth section, which cryptically expresses "13 under 13," three strings imitate a consort of viols in a funereal *Pavana lachrymae.* The music contains a quotation of the opening of Schubert's String Quartet in D minor (*Death and the Maiden*). A violin punctuates the dirge with insect-like sounds. The seventh section is the central threnody, "Black Angels!" References to the numbers 7 and 13 are abundant, and the strings imitate the "devil's trill" of Tartini's violin sonata of this title.

Bibliography

Music of the Twentieth Century, Chapter 15.

Discography

New York String Quartet. Composers Recordings CRI SD 283 (1972).

The Avant-Garde String Quartet in the U.S.A. Concord String Quartet. Vox SVBX 5306 (1973).

Gaudeamus String Quartet. Philips 6500 881 (1974).

(1) Crumb's life and influences

(2) Black Angels as a concept; form (comprised of 13 sections divided into 3 parts.)

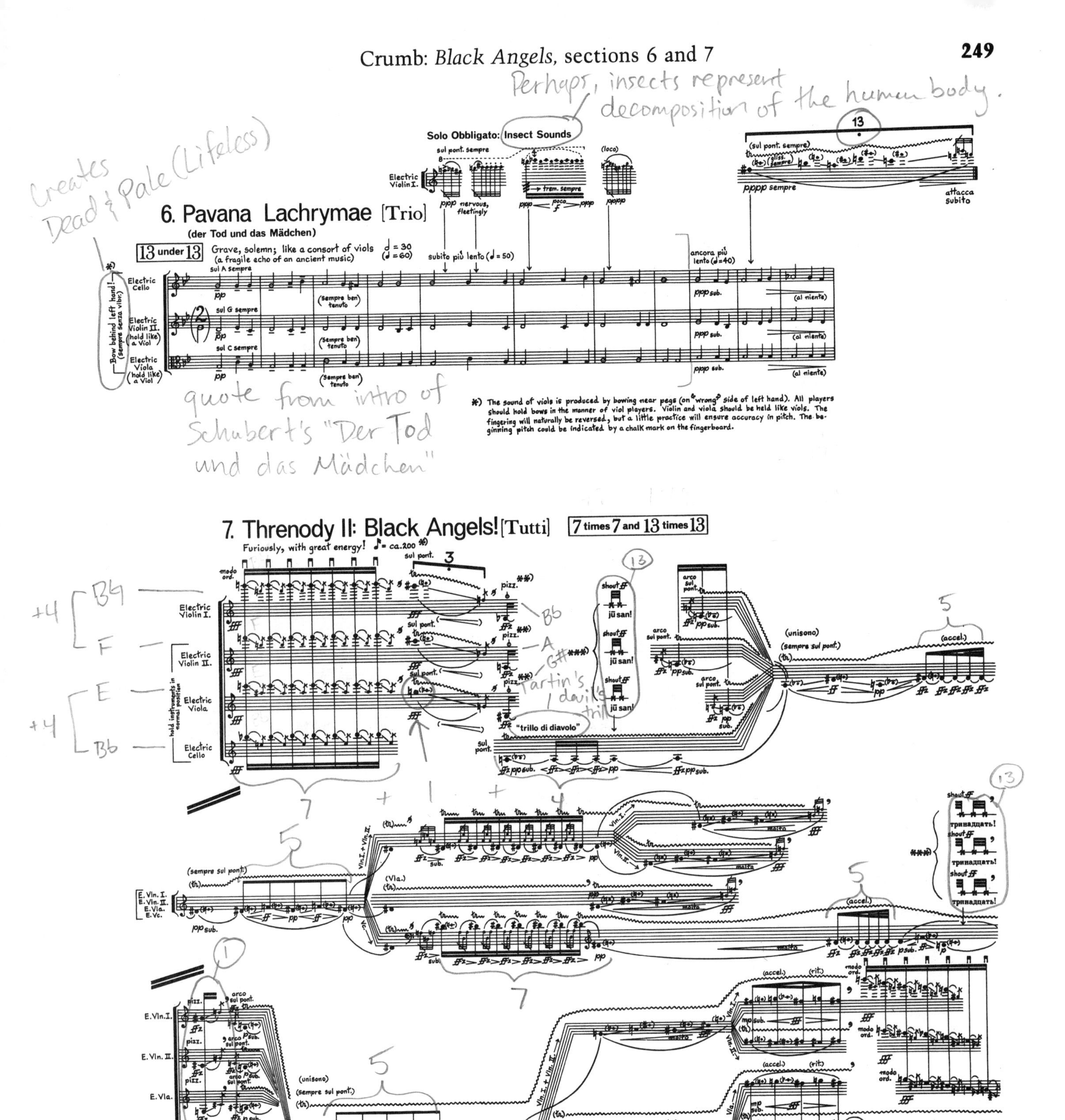

*) This piece should be performed in a very free manner. However, all precisely indicated durations should be approximately in tempo.

**) ♪ = a percussive pizzicato

***) The numeral thirteen in Japanese, Russian, and Swahili. Pronounce: Joo-sahn, Tree-naht'-saht, Koo-me'nah'tah-too (' = slight pause between syllables)

Copyright © 1971 by C. F. Peters Corporation. Used by permission.

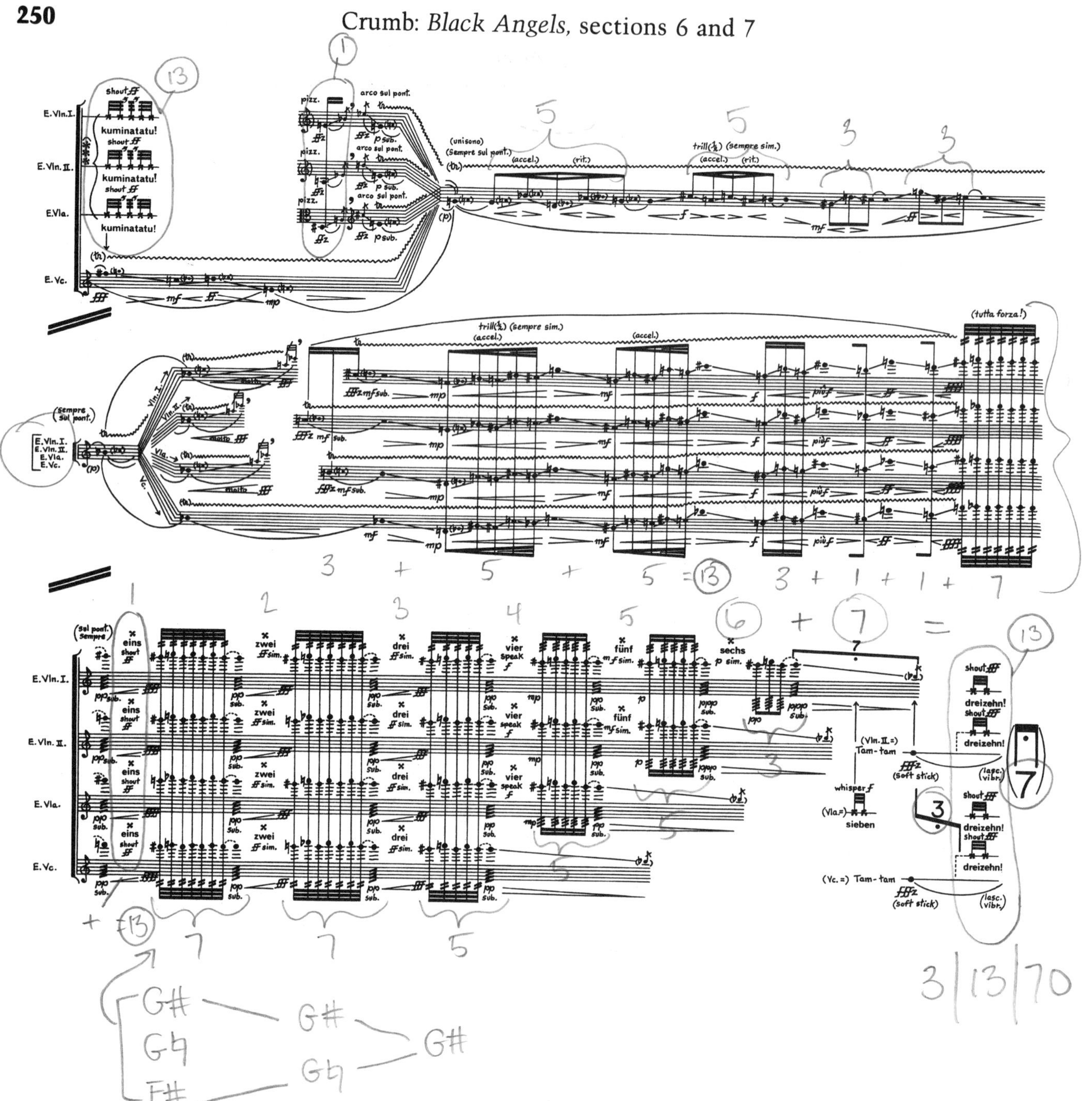
E. Vln. I.
E. Vln. II.
E. Vla.
E. Vc.
shout
kuminatatu!
pizz.
arco sul pont.
p sub.
(unisono)
(Sempre sul pont.)
(accel.)
(rit.)
trill (sempre sim.)
(Sempre sul pont.)
molto
(tutta forza!)
più f
(Sul pont. Sempre)
eins
zwei
drei
vier
speak
fünf
sechs
sieben
whisper
(Vln. II =) Tam-tam
(soft stick)
(lasc. vibr.)
(Vc. =) Tam-tam
dreizehn!

Steve Reich (1936–)

Clapping Music *(1972)*

Clapping Music is the last of Reich's "phase" compositions—in an idiom that occupied him from 1965. In phase music, two or more like-sounding instruments or tape tracks begin in unison sounding a continuously repeated figure. The lines then move out of phase, which produces new rhythmic and melodic fragments by the interaction of parts.

In *Clapping Music,* the two lines do not move gradually out of phase. The second performer instead leaps abruptly at the beginning of each measure an eighth note ahead of the first performer. The piece ends when the two performers have returned to unison.

Bibliography

Music of the Twentieth Century, Chapter 16.

Reich, Steve. "Notes on Composition 1965–1973." In *Writings About Music,* pp. 49–71. New York and Halifax, 1974.

Schwarz, K. Robert. "Steve Reich: Music as a Gradual Process." *Perspectives of New Music,* 19 (1980–81), 373–94; 20 (1981–82), 225–86.

Directions for Performance

The number of repeats is fixed at 12 repeats per bar. The duration of the piece should be approximately 5 minutes. The second performer should keep his or her downbeat where it is written, on the first beat of each measure and not on the first beat of the group of three claps, so that the downbeat always falls on a new beat of the unchanging pattern. No other accents should be made. It is for this reason that a time signature of 6/4 or 12/8 is not given – to avoid metrical accents. To begin the piece one player may set the tempo by counting quietly; "one, two, three, four, five, six".

The choice of a particular clapping sound, i.e. with cupped or flat hands, is left up to the performers. Whichever timbre is chosen, both performers should try and get the same one so that their two parts will blend to produce one overall resulting pattern.

In a hall holding 200 people or more the clapping should be amplified with either a single omni-directional microphone for both performers, or two directional microphones; one for each performer. In either case the amplification should be mixed into mono and both parts fed equally to all loudspeakers. In smaller live rooms the piece may be performed without amplification. In either case the performers should perform while standing as close to one another as possible so as to hear each other well.

© Copyright 1980 by Universal Edition (London) Ltd., London. All rights reserved. Used by permission of European American Music Distributors Corporation, sole U.S. agent for Universal Edition.

♩ = 160-184 Repeat each bar 12 times

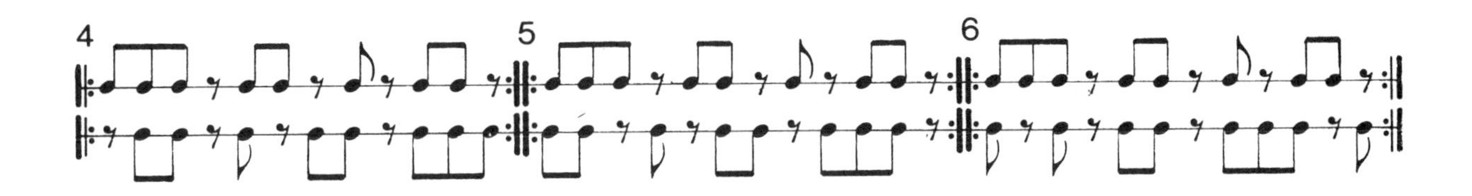

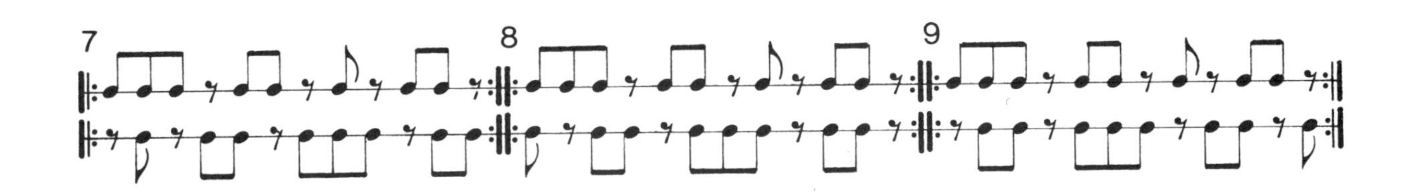

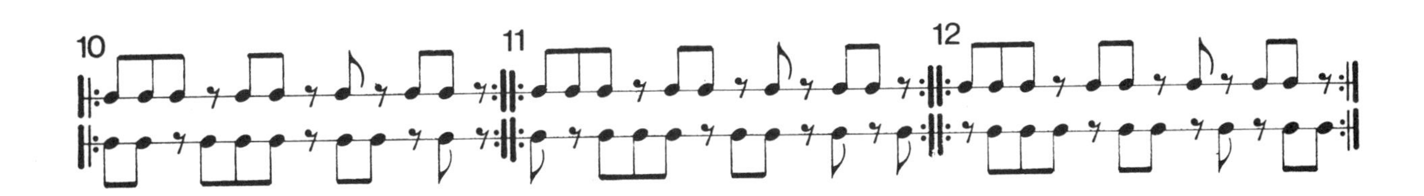

13

12/72

◆ 29 ◆

George Rochberg (1918-   )

Sixth String Quartet (1978): Third Movement (Variations [on Pachelbel])

George Rochberg's Sixth String Quartet is the last of three *Concord* quartets, named after the group for which they were written. These pieces continue the eclecticism of Rochberg's Third String Quartet in which styles from the baroque to the twentieth century are mingled and in which tonality and lyricism are unabashedly revived. Rochberg pays special homage in these quartets to Beethoven, Mahler, Berg, and Bartók.

The Sixth String Quartet is in five movements whose centerpiece is the Variations (on Pachelbel). This movement takes the form of baroque variations: continuous variations, that is, upon a four-measure bass line and descending melodic figure, both of which are drawn from the celebrated Canon in D major by Johann Pachelbel (1653-1706).

The style of the variations is decidedly flexible, as it begins in the manner of a baroque trio sonata and moves by measure 49 to the impassioned language of Mahler and early Schoenberg.

Bibliography

Music of the Twentieth Century, Chapter 15.

Discography

Concord String Quartet. RCA ARL2 4198 (1982).

© 1979 Theodore Presser Company. Used by permission of the publisher.

15
V. I
V. II
Va.
C.
p
cresc. poco a poco
20
mf

25
Vl. I
Vl. II
Va.
C.
arco
30
cantando

35
V. I
V. II
Va.
C.
mp
p
40

45
Un poco più mosso; e con molto calore
V.I
V.II
Va.
C.
sim.
mp
Pizz.
arco
cresc. molto
a tempo e molto espansivo
50
intensivo

V.I
V.II
Va.
C.
Rallentando
Poco adagio
molto espr.
molto espr.
cresc.
cresc.
55
Ritardando
molto dim.
dim.
molto dim.
molto espr.
molto dim.

Adagio
V.I
V.II
Va.
C.
dolciss.
poco
60
Subito a tempo (Poco andante)
e molto rubato
pizz.
arpegg.
a tempo
hold back
65
poco
cresc.
largo

a poco più mosso
Rit.
V.I
V.II
Va.
C.
poco a poco
dim.
a tempo
70
cresc.
L'istesso tempo; but with
the feeling of a slow march

75
V. I
V. II
Va.
C.
80

85
V. I
V. II
Va.
C.
sempre pp
sempre ppp
sempre pp
sempre pp
90
95